ORDINARILY SACRED

ORDINARILY SACRED

Lynda Sexson

University Press of Virginia   *Charlottesville and London*

THE UNIVERSITY PRESS OF VIRGINIA
Copyright © 1992 by the Rector and Visitors
of the University of Virginia

First published 1982 copyright © by Lynda Sexson
First paperback edition published 1992
Second printing 1993

Library of Congress Cataloging-in-Publication Data

Sexson, Lynda.
  Ordinarily sacred / by Lynda Sexson.
    p.   cm — (Studies in religion and culture)
  Originally published: New York : Crossroad, 1982.
  ISBN 0-8139-1416-7 (pbk.)
  1. Holy, The.   2. Experience (Religion)   3. Imagination—Religious
aspects.   4. Symbolism   5. Myth.   I. Title.   II. Series: Studies
in religion and culture (Charlottesville, Va.)
  [BL48.S48   1992]
  291.4'2—dc20
                                                    92-12892
                                                        CIP

Printed in the United States of America

For my grandmother,
Laura,
who shaped chaos into soul

Acknowledgments:

I am indebted to the many persons who have told me their stories and given time to mine, who have shown me their little things and a little of themselves. Earlier versions of two of these chapters have appeared in *Parabola: Myth and the Quest for Meaning,* and in *Perspectives in Art.* My sincere thanks to Adrienne Mayor and Nina Morris-Farber for their editorial guidance. I am especially grateful to Richard Payne, for his maieutic sensitivities. To Devin and Vanessa, for their dreams and laughter, and to Michael, for the texture, I am most thankful.

Contents

Introductory Note

Improvising may be the religious ritual and thought of the contemporary world. The interplay of old and new is at once iconoclastic and remythologizing. Religion—whether we choose to name the experience thus or not—is to be lured by the transitory that reveals the transcendent, to be captured by the aesthetic that discloses the divine word, and it is to mingle those categories so that, ultimately an integrative play cancels discrimination and makes obsolete or meaningless divisions between sacred and profane. The things of this world are vessels, entrances for stories; when we touch them or tumble into them, we fall into their labyrinthine resonances. The world is no longer divided then, into those inconvenient categories of subject and object, and the world becomes religiously apprehended.

Religion, like the meaning of life or a good joke, defies definition or explanation. But like these two, heightening awareness enriches the experience. To talk about religion in some sense is to practice it. Certainly my colleagues and I have had to make clear over and over, "the practice of religion and the study of religion are not the same thing." Yet for the present we must look at the reverse of that maxim and see that the study of religion may well be also a means of practicing it: to call up for reflection the nature of religion is itself a religious activity.

1

The angels are given to laughter when they see us sit down and attempt to talk about the nature of religion; but surely they themselves have given over eons to the pleasure of that very discussion.

This book attempts to illuminate the sacred quality of experience which on the surface is considered mundane or secular. In order to do so, I have drawn upon the most slender and ephemeral of our everyday experiences, which nevertheless resonate with the most profound of religious symbols. This is the work and nature of metaphor, a quality of experience manifested here by the little things we save—the "stuff" in children's boxes, by the things we say that get repeated—our texts of our lives, by our jokes and our dreams, by the way we play. It is not that the natural is an analogue for the spiritual, nor is it that the spiritual dwells pantheistically within the natural; it is, rather, that nature, spirit, or any other category is perceived and conceived through mind as metaphor. This means that there can be, ultimately, no formal separation of art from life, or of religion from culture.

Initially, we may be reluctant to muddle the borders of those discrete categories, the sacred and the profane, until we look back at three interrelated elements of our cultural heritage: the problem of radical dualism, deeply infused in our understanding of reality; the flux of iconoclasm and image-making, the core of western religious consciousness; and metaphor, the base and creator of any of these.

Religion, for this conversation, is concerned with individual insight and vision rather than with institutions and their histories. If we take seriously the religious experiences of founders, reformers, and mystics, then we may want to look at religion before it is codified and legitimated by its culture. The religious thoughts and intuitions of the great religious leaders cannot easily be studied outside of the interpretative contexts of their subsequent adherents and histories. One of the ways that we might inquire after the religious impulses of great innovators is to look at the religious impulses of persons who have made little or no impact on religious history—ourselves, ordinary individuals. Religions, unlike some of their heroes, are not born of virgins; they come from a context, a mingling of ideas, events, and images. Like their heroes, though, religions may first appear in temples or on mountainsides, or even in unlikely stables.

Although this discussion is concerned with individual experience, it is concerned with the contexts those experiences arise from and mingle with. There are no inherently sacred objects, events, or thoughts; they are made sacred by a special context. The usual, recognizable context of the sacred is an institutional or traditional setting through which the culture agrees that something has sacred content. What about those special—or metaphorically saturated—contents that burst out of traditional confines, or never find their way into them? If there is no political body to verify occurrences or images as religious or sacred, would these particularized events or images still have special connotations? Might we call that "sacred" or this "religious"? Without referring to those overwhelming, transforming experiences that occur somewhat rarely in human life, there are universal experiences which are common yet set apart, ordinary yet consummately extraordinary, mundane yet sacred. Since religion or the sacred cannot be confined by the categories implied in the divisions, "the sacred and the profane" or "the secular and the religious," this book seeks the religious profanely (outside the temple).

The sacred, when not bound up by politics and economics, is nearer to something we call the aesthetic. Both the religious and the aesthetic are informed by and produce an effect on the worldviews from which they arise. In some sense then, art and religion can be described as the notation of moments which discover or rediscover one's worldview, create or re-create one's philosophical depth. Art is the creation of an imaginative universe. Religion is the creation of an imaginative (or imaginal) universe—and the entering into the creation. Peculiar moments in ordinary lives, saturated by metaphor or personal symbol-making, are the stuff of religion.

The sacred quality of our lives is fabricated from the metaphors we make. We can discover or recognize the sacred within the secular, or the divine in the ordinary. We might say that our religious dilemma is not a secularizing dilemma but a "poetic" one. The following chapters contain intentional lacunae (holes, or riddles) making spaces for the reader's responses, memories, stories; they look at the unrecognized quality of our ordinary and spontaneous metaphors, from our clichés to our collections, from our play to our dreams.

1

Boxes
Improvising the Sacred

What is the distance between beads of dogwood berries a little girl strung and hid in a box under her bed, telling her own great-grandchild about them seventy years later, and the beads of the rosary developed as a memory guide for a series of prayers that have been used by generations since at least the fifteenth century? The distance between the dogwood berries and the rosary—between the improvised and the articulated—is indeed vast; but they are strung like beads along the same continuum of experience.

Inventories from children's hiding places and from religious holy places bear a remarkable similarity: bones, bright stones, beads, fur, feathers, bits of writing, nuts, a picture; or relics, *urim* and *thummim,* the borrowed power of the totemic animal, the regenerative grain, the sacred text, the host, the icon. Why do children collect feathers, hide gold paper, delicately perch a marble in the arms of an unresisting house plant, or stick shells under their beds or stones into their mattresses? The "junk" that is precious to children—and to adults—is precisely the stuff of the sacred.

Religion does not reside in these literal things but resides in them metaphorically. By metaphor, I mean the imaginal reality that gives depth and integrity to our lives. *Imaginal* means not merely the *imaginative* (as in referring to works of art) and certainly not the *imaginary* (as in referring to silly things made up); the imaginal makes up the world. For example, one might consider *The Divine Comedy* to be an imaginative work, populated with some imaginary beings, which has contributed to the imaginal world of western consciousness. Looking at boxes and into boxes, looking at sacred urns, arks, vessels of religious traditions, but more particularly at the ephemera of more mundane circumstances, we will elicit the notion of the sacred metaphor. Finally, to distinguish from the sentimental and the monumental, we can identify the sacred as residing within the metaphorical dynamic rather than within any object.

Human experience and thought can be charted as profoundly by records of image-making as by war-making, by the keeping of stories as by the keeping of boundaries. Though we may often call this image-making power the imaginal, or perhaps symbolic structure, metaphor, or even a minimal mysticism, we must choose sometimes to call it religion. Whatever term it is given, it is in danger of being diminished, stuck into the wrong conceptual category, or denied.

My son once found the hip-bone of a large cow. He wore it as a stately garment or as armor; he played the bone like a guitar or played himself in the bone like a dinosaur. He circulated his interest upon the bone back into his discovery of it in the woods, to the being who had walked it before abandoning it, to the shape and feel of it, to hanging it on the wall and looking at it and the shadows it cast. And the bone was transformed—quite beyond the original fragment of decay in the woods—into images of everything from death to art. As my child played upon his guitar a song I could not quite hear, I wondered just how far play was from religion.

Religion is a confusing, perhaps distorting term; and if religion or the sacred is to be discovered or reaffirmed in this culture, it will have to be found under the bed, in the box, like a string of dogwood berries upon which the rosary of a life can be sung.

Religion is not a discrete category within human experience; it is rather a quality that pervades all of experience. Accustomed as we are to distinguishing between "the sacred" and "the profane," we fail to remember that such a dividing up of reality is itself a religious idea. It is often an awkward idea, rather like someone trying to carry himself over a stream in his own arms—a confusion of part and whole, form and function. There are no inherently religious objects, thoughts, or events; in contemporary culture so much of our world has been "contaminated" with the *mundane* we hardly recognize a quality of the sacred. This has been called the process of secularization or of modernization, but it may be something else, it may be a nearly inevitable consequence of a dualistic paradigm, a religious point of view that divides reality into two. Indeed, the words *mundane*—of the world, *profane*—outside the temple, and *secular*—of the temporal, indicate that whatever is "before the temple" is made of space and time (mundane and secular) and whatever is not of the world and temporality is that which is contained within the category of the sacred. However, that arrangement of reality means not only that *material* events and knowledge are devalued, but that *events* and *knowledge* altogether are devalued and deprived of the quality of the sacred.

Someone holding to a dualistic worldview—the religious premise that divides reality into matter and spirit—must "eat the angel's portion." The vegetables are added, the fine spices blended, but the angel dines only upon the steam that escapes when the lid is removed. An altogether glorious meal for angels, but authentic dualists cannot even savor the steam—infused as it is with the aroma and flavor of the mundane.

And, oddly, however much of the old dualistic religion has been cast off by contemporary consciousness, the structure of its worldview has remained; the old belief system may have fallen away, but its division of reality persists. People who assert, "Religious? oh, I'm not very," have unwittingly affirmed the basis of the system they claim to reject.

How else, we might ask, can we express the spiritual—or our experience that seems to transcend the limits of ordinary space and time? A quick inventory back inside the temple reveals that the holy is made up of words and works identical to all the stuff of the profane world. The sacred boxes are filled with things and ideas pirated or spirited away from the profane world, just as a five-year-old boy once carried the cow bone out of the woods and into his imagination.

Dualistically organized religions, no matter how iconoclastic their impulses, keep "suffering" from infusions of the metaphor—and because the dualistic mind confuses the metaphorical with the literal, the absurd sets in. There is a story typical of the ninth century, when the cult of relics was gaining prominence in Christian worship, concerning a fraud. According to Bishop Theoboldus,

> last year two individuals claiming to be monks brought what they said were the bones of a saint which they claimed to have carried off from Rome or from some other part of Italy. The name of the saint they claimed, with amazing impudence, to have forgotten. . . . [Nevertheless] in the church, women fell and writhed as though buffeted by some outside force although no visible signs of injuries appeared.[1]

The relic fraud offers an example of the collision of the literal mind with conceptual dualism; the metaphorical element absent, the women writhe before fake bones and the bishop writhes before their gullibility. (Perhaps it would be fairer to suppose that at least some of the women engage in a higher fraud—that of knowing what they "do not know"—and thus participate in a metaphorical reality after all.)

How is it, then, that thinking and things are made holy or sacred? Perhaps a clue can be gleaned from the words themselves: etymologically *holy*—wholeness, and *sacred*—to be consecrated, set apart and purified, may indicate that the dualism that divides the world into the sacred and the profane, or the holy and the ordinary, actually undercuts or eradicates the holy (wholeness) since *all* reality must be—or is potentially—sacred (consecrated).

Religion, then, is the consecration of experience, or person, so that the person, or experience, is made whole (holy). Religion may be an unfortunate term (some cultures have no equivalent for this word),[2] a term that should refer to becoming so intimate with space (the mundane) and time (the secular) that they—or we—are transformed by consciousness and made holy. Religion is more a quality of perceiving and knowing than it is of bowing before the bizarre.

If religion is to be found, it may be discovered under the bed—in the box under the bed. That is, religious "boxes" are not to be considered literal containers, but psychic ones. The box is a space that folds other spaces into itself.

If religion is in the box under the bed, it is not something like outgrown clothes, not a cultural neurosis.

If religion is in the box under the bed, it is not something like old diaries, full of discarded, quaint, or antiquarian interests—religion does not necessarily belong to the childhood of humanity.

Although under the bed, religion is not like balls of lint—well, perhaps it does resemble balls of lint:

When I was three years old, we moved into a little house and my mother set about cleaning. I watched. Her broom disrupted seemingly animated toys that scuttled out from under the bed.

I wanted to keep them.

"No," said my mother. "They're just dirt. Lint balls."

"I could play with them. They look like animals."

"No."

Then something else slid out from under the bed by the force of my mother's broom. It was a marvelously decrepit little book, wonderful enough to give pause to my mother's purification ritual. She sat with me on the bed and showed me page by page, image by image, "Look, here is a picture drawn by a girl seven years old. It says this one is by a boy five years old, another by a boy four-and-a-half." They were all pictures of people, drawn by children, bound in a book.

It was an extraordinary moment. I suddenly had all these friends to draw with; my mother had stopped sweeping and was talking about drawing, giving it moment and import; I was going to place my drawings with theirs. We reached the last page and I reached for the book.

"No, you can't have it. It's too dirty; I have to throw it away."

And the taboo book joined the fuzz-ball animals. But the book (or the moment, the occasion of the book and my mother) stayed somewhere within me; and sometimes the most likely place to find religion is in an unlikely place—under the bed with the dust mice.

∽

Overcoming a dualistic heritage (however strongly those dualistic presuppositions seem to belong to religious knowledge) brings one into the sphere in which ordinary reality is saturated with the sacred. Religion is made up of nothing special—the ordinary is holy or potentially holy; since the object of the religious is no-thing, its images can be improvised from oatmeal boxes and sand sculpture. The apprehension of the sacred is manifested in an imaginal relationship with the divine—reinventing the *ordinarily sacred*.

Another scan of contents and contours within the temple reveal how the holy is made: from the ephemera and scraps of the ordinary world by means of metaphor.

As Kafka's aphorism tells us,

> Leopards break into the temple and drink the sacrificial chalice dry; this occurs repeatedly, again and again: finally it can be reckoned on beforehand and becomes part of the ceremony.[3]

Now we would ask Kafka for a parable in which there is no temple, no established ceremony or sacrificial vessel, but one in which leopards nevertheless surprise us by appearing and drinking from our cups. Leopards breaking in—upon whatever our complacencies—is the nature of religion. We long for a reappearance of Kafka himself to break in and tell us that mysterious thing we need to know about religion: religion as leopards drinking from—if not our sacred vessels—then whatever cups we have in hand.

The shock of leopards, even if they can be reckoned on beforehand, even if they are a part of the ceremony, is religion. The intrusions of the "mundane" become agents of the sublime. They are incorporated—"bodied" into the divine. Thus the containers: the chalices, temples, ceremonies, memories, predictions, words and works, envelop the shock and become associated with the sacred.

In searching out the sacred, then, within the context of a residual dualism, one must examine what has been overlooked. Several years ago I was introduced to an old man who lived in a mountainous, abandoned village that had briefly housed a small mining industry. The people had retreated, died, or moved on, leaving him to his summers of paradise and winters so deeply snowed no one could travel in or out. His mountain contained him and he contained the memory of that brief village, whose houses were decaying around his own well-tended one.

The old man shared his sauna, his hospitality. And to introduce himself he granted me a tour of his carved, curved-glass china cabinet. "This was my wife's," he said as he turned the little key. Her "box"—I could see at a glance—had been readjusted, still evoking her memory, but now invoking his own as well.

He showed me the European china and silver spoons that spoke as eloquently as his accent of the heritage they had abandoned, and the little bits of it, the presence of their past, they could carry with them. In tonalities of thought and expression, in silver spoons and delicate china, the distant space and time were made present. These had been his wife's, invested more with her imaginal reality than his own; by her death she was invoked through them; and what had been her memory chambers, the contents of her heritage "box," became chambers of herself in his memory container. He placed a cup in my hand, and I held his fragile memory of that woman and her own memory of another land.

He showed me great gleaming chunks of ore, teaching me how to recognize the genuine thing, making jokes about fools and their gold. There were rumors, he would say, sometimes generated by himself for his own amusement, that he had great chests and safes filled with gold bars, mined and refined by himself, that were worthless. Governmental control of the economy forbade him to sell them—"they" didn't want the gold. So there he was, with a kingly treasure made worthless by that strange bureaucracy that held him captive. His "box" of gold— whether physically verifiable or not—was a mysterious treasure that had no external value, as with the alchemists who sometimes claimed the treasure was worthless to the outside world. Like the mining life that had dried up and left him stranded in a perfect and "worthless" place, his gold could not be cashed in. Although non-dualistic religion will break down the artificial barriers between the sacred and the profane, it nevertheless will distinguish among the various forms of recognition (or nonrecognition) of the sacred.

The old man showed me little trinkets, honored among the china, things I imagined his wife would not have permitted in that cabinet, but things he liked because they were memory guides to family, to neighbors, to his own solitary experience. Ugly ceramics representing decades of popular whimsy had become in his china cabinet a record of an interiorized past. Their amusements still held for him, and he stored within them his own humor and affection.

Also in the cabinet were objects he had found; melting snow leaves as rich a beach as departing tide. Around his house, as around many beach houses, fragments of nature and civilization marked his boundaries and discoveries. The worthless, the lost, and the abandoned, became the reinvented. Pieces of wood and painted tin, a jar, decorated iron, marked the edges of his own space and counted the seasons of his being.

He told us of his next door neighbor, my friend's grandfather. When we returned to the little house we had played in, that the grandfather had once lived and worked in, what was the nature of that container? And how did we feel when we examined the lasts in the box that the grandfather had used to make shoes? And how did our children feel, exploring abandoned houses, looking inside ornate iron ranges, into closets at scraps of wallpaper and catalogues, climbing into the rusted skeletons of old cars? Did they sense that these were "boxes," or that human life is transitory, its artifacts therefore poignant? No, the children found their own mysteries and took on their own meanings; no loss, but as on the beach or after melting snow, there was discovery.

⌒

If religion is defined by institutions, one may make the error of identifying the familiar rather than uncovering the mystery. Early Christians were called atheists because they had no temples, no iconic representations, no sacrifices. Many religions are named by outsiders rather than by those within their systems. From the inside religion seems to be the focus for what it means to be human; from the outside religions seem to suggest that it is questionable whether those "others" are fully human. The collective term "religion" does not refer to a specialized category, but to the way that all reality is perceived and integrated.

We sometimes pretend that the religious institution contains the spiritual investment of its entire community; but when the institution fails, we may then be confused into thinking that religion has failed, or is lost.

To look at religion—at the imaginal—one must find the "box" under the bed. Certainly religious meaning cannot be contained in a box, but the "box" is an admission that meaning "shows itself" in our lives. The box may be—larger than a breadbox, even the breadbox itself—the resting place of the host; it may be a room, a house, a cathedral, or the City of God or the Vision of Heaven. Some of the boxes that will draw our attention already have been perceived as containers of the sacred; others are the boxes that anyone except the owner, and perhaps even the owner, would say contain junk. These are the sacred possessions opaque to all but the memory of the owner. These are the things that are thrown out when people move, die, go to college, or change their minds about who they are. The box may be anything from Nicholas of Cusa's mystical circle to a map of the universe, from a cartoon to a kiss, from an aquarium to a quilt.

One of the most prominent sacred boxes in the history of religions is the Ark of the Covenant of the ancient Hebrews. Speculation about the ark has led to suggestions that it contained sacred serpents, ancestral bones, or other sanctified relics, cultic objects, oracular devices, images, or texts. The pious tradition tells us that it held the tablets of the Ten Commandments, the pot of manna, and Aaron's rod.

The Ark of the Covenant disappears from the cult, but its stories remain in the tradition. Indeed, Richard of St. Victor, in the twelfth century, meditating upon the priestly instructions for the construction of the Ark, composed a treatise, "The Mystical Ark,"[4] delineating his six degrees of contemplation, for which he became famous as *Magnus Contemplator.* He accomplished his work about contemplation, however, by himself performing a great work of contemplation, or what we generally call meditation. He built a box. Referring to the instructions of Exodus 25, Richard translated the literal measurements, materials, and design into theological analogues so that wood, gold, human experience, and divine meaning are one in the building of the Ark.

Before the work is begun, Richard reminds his readers that they already know the secret he is about to painstakingly construct, that the Ark—for his allegorically minded readers and himself—is Christ. As the Ark is built, the universe is recreated and divine meaning is revealed.

The Ark, like any geometrical box, has length, width, and height. Richard names the length of the Ark "the consideration of things," the width the "consideration of works," and the height the "consideration of morals." The length of the box, "things," is made up of matter and form—or nature. In that single line, before the box has taken form, Richard has room enough to pack up all the "things" of the natural world. The width of the box is measured by the works of human activity, which we see in "pictures, carvings, books, and similar things," and in nature, "that herbs and trees grow; that they produce flowers and fruit."

The box is so far only a plane figure without depth, yet there is already room enough to pack all the fruits of the human imagination as well as of natural time. Finally, through morals, or "human instructions and divine instructions," the figure acquires dimension and depth, becoming a geometric solid, a box that can contain the "hidden place of divine secrets."

Following the instructions in Exodus, Richard allegorically gilds the Ark on the outside with the physical causes of things; he gilds the interior with the rational principle of justice. One side of the Ark is for things made by the workings of God, and the other is for things that happen by the permission of God. Richard even built into the corners of the Ark the negative aspects of experience.

Rings were attached to the Ark, according to the Exodus blueprint, through which the carrying rods should be inserted. These rings are named God's fourfold wisdom; and the figure of the ring itself, which is "turned back upon itself," evokes for Richard, as it has for generations of mystics and poets, an image and idea of which "neither beginning nor end can be found in it." The suspension of the Ark of Sanctification by these rings permits it to be "carried about in any direction without any deviation of error." And by means of Richard's contemplative carpentry, we suddenly apprehend the objects in our minds made by the master craftsmen—Bezaleel of the Bible and Richard of St. Victor—a stunning mandala of perfection. Not only is the circle squared, the cube is sphered. The motion of the universe itself moves Richard's Ark, and that motion incorporates the churning of Ezekiel's wheels as well as the turning of the seasons—perhaps even the changing of a mind.

Yet the Ark is not completed. It must be graced by cherubim, made completely of beaten gold, transcending the "wood" of history and nature. It is the angelic form we must assume "if we wish to fly to contemplation of eternal and divine things."

Richard performs another act of theological geometry as he places the crown on the Ark:

> It is flat with regard to those things which are according to reason;
> concave with regard to those which are beyond reason;
> pierced with regard to those which seem to be against reason.[5]

The allegory for Richard is not a sham construction, or simply a pointing toward the truth beyond; the allegory is as "real" as history and nature. "Why do you marvel that allegory is woven into history in a marvelous manner?" he asks, describing the ingenious gold engravings overlaying the wood of his Ark. "The symbol," for Richard, "is not an abstract representation of ideas; it is, rather, a concrete manifestation of truth."[6]

Is the mystical Ark of this great contemplative mind really cousin to the box under a seven-year-old's bed, who does not speculate about the contents but names it merely "my good stuff"? Not if we mean by "symbol" the pointing toward an abstraction, a feeble figuration of a noble idea. But if we mean by "symbol" something closer to what Richard of St. Victor meant when he rebuilt the Ark of the Covenant—that is, the re-presentation or the making in the world or in the world of the mind, an embodiment of the divine—then Richard's grandly conceived Ark and the child's ephemera correspond. The "good stuff" is, in some uncanny way, comparable to Richard of St. Victor's finely wrought Ark.

⌒

Someone will ultimately complain, "If the divine is made manifest in a collection of flotsam, isn't this just a perversely contrary idolatry, confusing the wastes of space and time with the truth of eternity?" Following fast upon Someone's complaint, her brother will ask, "Yes, but if everything is *potentially* a 'box' or sacred storehouse, how do we recognize it? If everything is sacred, nothing is. Or, how can we decide that one kid's pocket is filled with divine objects and another's is just trouble for the washer?"

We must, indeed, be able to distinguish among the sentimental, the nostalgic, the trivial, and the truly religious. Religion is the desire for depth. It is the experience or expression of the world imagined. Religion is not in the sentimental nor the monumental; yet these two always attach themselves to the religious. The one reduces the religious impulse to the manageable, the second puffs it, seals it, codifies it. In both instances the religious imperative—the depth metaphor—is diminished or erased. It is apparently an easy error to monumentalize or sentimentalize rather than to experience the metaphorical or imaginal. The error is common within as well as without ecclesiastical protections. Religion is not in souvenirs or memorials, but they seem to be found in spots designated as sacred acreage or in fragments of it pocketed away.

I once knew a woman with three possessions: alligator shoes, a player piano, and a parrot (her former companion), dead, stuffed, perched and dusty among the potted plants. Music, exotic animals, and her own thwarted friendship, were turned inside out to mechanical, manageable toys (although she ended up giving away the tight scaly shoes, selling the silenced piano, and giving up the ghost before being forced into a decision regarding the deteriorating parrot husk). Sentimentality claimed her.

The monumental is in ecclesiastical or civil edifices and ceremonies that inflate the obvious or drain the metaphor and "set it in stone." Museums frequently squat as monuments that artificially sacralize, born of an impulse to provide for material culture what religious monuments attempt for the spiritual.

Everyone has at some time been coerced to stand quietly before political points-of-view (as before individual names marking the spots where white soldiers fell, and designations for "Indian" where rebellious reds died); or people have paid their coins to find the sentimental grotesquely monumentalized, or even the grotesque monumentally sentimentalized. Makeshift museums curated by nothing more than the random, capricious generosity of a surrounding community line up visitors to admire a clutter of mementos: pictures and notices of the tallest woman who came this way; bones of Indians and Chinese along with the "petrified" remains of an unfortunate cat found under a porch, and a snake skin, leveling them all to similar curiosities; the oval-framed portrait of a settler who made some money from his garden produce and watched a famous hanging; and the centerpiece, the foot of Clubfoot George, bandit, enshrined in a bell-jar, pictures available on color postcards.

The contents, the specific objects, found among the sentimental and the monumental collections, are outwardly indistinguishable from objects that metaphorically participate in the sacred.

The great religious traditions have warned against attachment to things, even against noble attachments we might call love. Sometimes these admonitions come from a dualistic perspective which warns against the dark, the earthly, or unreality. But other times they warn against the parrot husk, not denying that all life is rolling inevitably toward decay, but warning against missing the point, of literalizing the metaphorical.

Jesus told the rich young man and the listeners to his parable that they must give up their wealth—their things—to follow him. A Buddhist parable tells of Gotami, whose child had died and left her in uncomprehending grief. The Buddha told her he would make medicine for her child if she would gather mustard seed from a house that death had not visited. Gotami, informed that death had preceded her at every house where she sought the medicine, at last understood and threw the corpse of her child and her attachment upon the burial pyre. These teachings thus express their opposition to the world; but even traditions that do not may nevertheless teach the relativity of the world. Chuang Tzu, the Taoist philosopher, the comic metaphysician, tells of a man who loved a courtesan with three eyes. After that, Chuang Tzu says, women with only two eyes seemed ugly—deficient in beauty.

The box cannot be literalized; the religious move is into metaphor. One of the Zen stories from the tradition of Dogen is a story about a monk who carried a box with him always. He burned incense before it "and showed his respect with salutations and offerings." The box contained a golden image of the Buddha and some relics.

The Zen Master told the monk that the contents of the box would be of no use to him, to give them up.

The monk objected.

Then the Zen Master said it was the handiwork of demons and to get rid of it.

The monk, angry, started to leave.

The Zen Master called out for the monk to open his box and look inside. The monk stopped, opened his box, and found, in place of the sacred treasures, a coiled, poisonous snake.

The sacred box is not literal; the things it holds cannot be held or seen by the insensitive; novices are not permitted to gaze upon the mysteries until they are prepared. Otherwise, comfortable idolatry or untranscending horror block the imaginal, the sacred.

Though religion is not in sentimental attachments or souvenirs, these can offer clues about the nature of religion. Even sentimental souvenirs can explode into the realm of the sacred. The sacred is the leopard lying in wait—the shock of its sudden appearance. Perhaps one of the most startling places the leopard can appear is among the ephemeral nonsense that distracts us into metaphor.

☞

Postcards made up from personal portraits and local sights were part of the ephemera of popular culture marking and making the transition into the twentieth century. It is as though those photograph greetings had only just now arrived, surprising us with what they have to say, providing another transition into the next century.

The original senders and recipients were celebrating their own senses of place and self-worth preserved in moments held ("Hold still!"), locking an embroidered collar, a steady gaze, a gloved hand, into the peculiar time of pasteboard image. On one side: the photograph, perhaps more mysterious to the giver than to the gifted, for being able to preserve in a photograph one's external self like the dolls of selves reflected in mirrors, in water, in another's eye, never sufficed. In the photograph the image held still, locked into a position that resembled eternity. On the other side: "Post Card. Address. Message." The subject forever still-lifed on the front, sent into motion on the back—destination, carrying one place to another. The archaic laws of mundane time and space, on front and back, defied. Cancelled, delivered.

Collected, preserved, or, as gratuitous survivors, a few have reached beyond their intended destinations and fallen into our contemporary hands. We must realize that although these flimsy prophets transcended the transient customs of space and time, as photographs they were intended as an image of forever, while as postcards they were never meant to last so long. The ones we see have outlasted their intentions; postcards are thin, temporary announcements. They announced the culmination of a mechanistic view of the world, an objectifying of reality. No one had much to add to that message—and in casual script with lead pencils they managed a "hello from here"; or, "here is a picture of the children it is not very good. We are all well and having a good time"; or, "We are having some rainy weather. with Love. Did not expect to have these taken that day"; or, "Sorry I did not have time to put your buggy in the barn"; or, "How are you? Why don't you ever write. Johnny is up today for the first time since he has been sick. He had the typhoid fever. He is half a head taller than Mama and is as thin as anything"; or, "Dear Papa, This is the grandest place I ever saw." They were messages mostly without ostensible content; the cards themselves are phatic communion, another metamorphosis of the valentine.

But when we pick them up, surprised that they've drifted into our current decade, that celebration of a world of "progress" made upon space and time is gone. The photographs, the messages, and the engraved profiles of George Washington which gave them their legitimate momentum, have subtly changed character. The stamps of Benjamin Franklin feature *putti* holding aloft lightbulbs—fake Renaissance and the American dream. The stamps spoke as well as the photographs to a world that had obliterated one common language and substituted another. The photograph spoke its own evocative language, taking the place of other description.

The photographs seem now not to have captured and sealed a particular moment in time but rather to have created a moment otherwise invisible. No one can see as the camera does, devoid of motion or the quality of change. Although we have inherited the mechanistic world and its conquering heroes, we are entering into a worldview once again more vital, more interrelated. We are moving in western culture from an object world toward process and connections. These old postcards, past their time and intent, have lost their status as sentimental objects and have become more like what in previous times were sometimes named Hermes, Iris, the Old Animal Wives, or Kothar-wa-Khasis: metaphors of crossing over barriers of subject and object, or time and its counterpoint. This time, the names are faint echoes—and what will we utter, how shall we call out to that experience of relatedness? For convenience (or for provocation) we'll name it religion, keeping in mind that this is the name for picking up an old postcard and looking at it.

At the age of ten I came upon an old postcard of that type and kept it privately. Each time the inventory of my psyche shifted, the card was still part of the lot, and each time I slipped it away, forgotten. And once my mother came to my own grown-up's house and happened upon that card, still with me. Her surprise startled me. "That's my card!" she said. "I've had it since I was a little girl." Somehow it had made its way along time as her treasure until a bandit had taken it. And who had been the keeper of the card before it became my little-girl mother's?

It was a photograph of a sand sculpture, a reclining madonna with her child in her arms, serenely awaiting the incoming tide. I used to look at the picture, at the woman lying serenely with her child's leg resting on her belly, with the inevitability of the tide that would come over her, already sounding under her bed. Why didn't she try to save the child, I'd think, but then realize—she, like him, is made of sand. This Madonna de la Mer, waiting to dissolve in a tide that had occurred and washed her away long before I or my mother was born, but ironically preserved on pasteboard, made me marvel about the transitory shapes of our eternal desires as much as any eloquence carved from marble.

The back of the postcard, written in pencil, said:

> Dear Mrs. Guye,
> You can put this with your curiosities. It was photographed from a picture made in the sand by a tramp. His only tools were his hands and a piece of drift wood. He goes along the beach making pictures, taking up a collection & going on and the tide obliterates his creations a friend of ours made this photo.
> We are having a good time.
> Fondly, Mrs. Young.

When I was a girl, I didn't like Mrs. Young, who no doubt has failed to resist time as well as her ephemeral message. Thinking her callous and ignorant to call an artist a tramp, I found her too easily impressed by his skill and too easily disdainful of his apparent social station. When I was older, I decided the sculpture was not sophisticated enough, a campy bit of an oddity. But I've come back round to seeing it—and I've come round to forgiving Mrs. Young, who sent me, *sub rosa*, this card.

Ah, Mrs. Young, didn't you think that you too would, like the tramp and his work, like your photographer and his work, dissolve? Or did you know that your bland pencil would preserve you, along with your tramp and his image, not into eternity, but into the sandy constructions of my own shoreline of consciousness? As for the artist, did you know that when nothing is left we come to art? Or, did you want to tell us that we make the sacred—the goddess—with whatever it is we have at hand, and that the eternal, in this realm, looks like sand?

The invisibility of the moment is the image of religion, or of art or of love. Another old postcard I have is part of a series in a courtship. This particular card is an ordinary, dull photograph of an island, but the message is another picture of the island, drawn with a rough, incapable hand, triangled boats and scribbled trees, labeled "love and kisses." The foolishness, the inadequacy, the redundancy, might say something of all of our arts, even our sacred ones, all of our feelings, even our profound ones.

c·ɔ

The box—or the sand sculpture—or the postcard—or the medicine bundle—cannot contain religion (religion being one's worldview which includes human life and the cosmos, art and ethic, thought and dream); yet the "box" is an admission that religious meaning "shows itself" via metaphor.

The box is the prevailing metaphor here because boxes or containers are so prevalent as sacred symbols. Containers in some instances have more metaphorical profundity than whatever they may house; or they embody by metaphor the unnameable or invisible holy.

Containers have housed the human soul. Moving to a new

house, giving birth, or going into battle might endanger the soul; and so, for safekeeping, it could be placed in a horn, the metal of a knife, a stone, a bag, until the danger was past. The souls of new babies were conjured into split coconuts in Borneo,[7] the coconuts sealed up and suspended from the roof as, it seems, soul wombs, until the baby's body should be a strong enough and safe enough "sacred container" for the soul.

Medicine bundles of the Plains Indians were made up of feathers, skulls, fur, things odd and ordinary. Often the contents were dreamed and then gathered in the daylight. That means, of course, not that the Native Americans were superstitious or primitive regarding their environment, but that the ordinary objects within medicine bundles were made of elements of dream consciousness. And if one's medicine bundle were considered particularly effective, it could be duplicated for a worthy friend. This indicates that the power lay not in a collection of specific contents, but in the consciousness by which they were gathered.

The religious traditions that have dominated the west have bequeathed to us a rigid distinction between the sacred and the secular. This dichotomy, which protects the authority of institutions, discredits the spontaneous, which has sacred potential. Politically organized religions manipulate sacred symbols in order to enhance and protect their "secular" or community authority. Tricked in our own cultural heritage by a dualism that denies the value of experience in the world, even by noble ideas such as the "separation of church and state," or by the human habit of demarcating and portioning out sacred areas, we can find ourselves pushed to the edge of reality—that no-place of liminality where the religious symbol can express its power. Since we gave up the antiquated notions of the unity of reality and the participatory animation of the physical world, we have lost our relationship to the world. Dualism, a more deterministic view, has remained in place.

Private Drive a hand-lettered board chats with the public that goes by. *This Is Not Garbage* written in felt-tip pen on the back of a cardboard pizza carton, leans against a philodendron in a "family restaurant," loudly protecting the plant from abuse in an abstract, dualistic world. *Flowers* a placard explains to the university traffic passing the tulips. *Caution: Scenic Vistas Ahead* we are told. Sometimes I think that I will raise a sign myself: *Beware of Stuff* or *Watch for Residue of Material Culture,* or *Caution: Muse Crossing.*

One of the religious perspectives that we have inherited in this secular age is an anti-materialistic world. No matter (and there is no matter) what the prophesying sandwich boards tell, the world is not doomed because of our lust for material. The culture that has thrown out its religious rituals and theologies remains firm in its dualistic metaphysics, despising the things of this world. Material may be hoarded or flaunted, but the hoarders and flaunters are genuine anti-materialists, spinning straw into glitter and starving, unable to find quality of experience, or what one might call poetic consciousness, or the imaginal. "Materialism" is evidence of the demonic among some cultural dualists; thus "the disposable" and "planned obsolescence" seem to free them from loving the world, while they await a Second Coming and negate ecological sensibilities. Without dualism, the material can be metaphorically valued without being literally idolized or despised.

Between the personal and the transpersonal is something like "making do," making up, or improvising. It is something like finding a poem or making a medicine bundle from a dream. One must be able to *look:* something attracts us ("Let me turn aside and see this great sight"); something causes us to reflect upon our own nature in relation to the transpersonal ("Take off your shoes"); and changes reality ("For you are on Holy Ground"); and reveals the transcendent ("I am I . . ."); and demands the transformation ("Go, . . .").

As metaphor empowers one discrete element of reality to mingle with another, religious metaphor pulls the artist into itself, too. More troublesome than the departure of the gods is the departure of their playful influence on human creativity, their infusion into human expression, their touching of human events and objects. The gods had to leave because they had been literalized and cut in two. Perhaps the only way into a greater mystery is through the meager, the minimal.

Julian of Norwich had an experience in which she found, in the palm of her hand something that was nearly nothing:

> And in this he showed me something small, no bigger than a hazelnut, lying in the palm of my hand, as it seemed to me, and it was as round as a ball. I looked at it with the eye of my understanding and thought: What can this be? I was amazed that it could last, for I thought that because of its littleness it would suddenly have fallen into nothing. And I was answered in my understanding: It lasts and always will, because God loves it; and thus everything has being through the love of God.[8]

One almost suspects that Julian's entire spiritual speculations and theology could have germinated with the seemingly quaint nutshell of her experience.[9] It was through this homely vision, with few links (but with subsequent applications) to the particular theological tradition in which she dwelt, in profound simplicity, of something like the "nothing" of a hazelnut in her hand, that there exploded in her the certitude of who she was in relation to God. Her amazement at that round, small thing, so inconsequential that it is remarkable that it is something rather than nothing, gives way to the deeper recognition that it is indeed nothing, appearing only by the grace of the only reality that is. Julian awoke to her God by looking at this little thing, "as round as a ball"; she came to know her theological universe as though it were a little hazelnut in her hand.

The box, the bundle, the hazelnut, are not objects but the interplay between self and universe, whereby the self originates poetic participation in the universe, and the universe is formed by that information.

2

Weaving Lies and Lives Together
The Making of Sacred Text

Were the old stories older when they were told long ago? Did they reach deeper and connect more intimately with the listeners in the time when their text was con-textual? Did Trickster pale when he was kidnapped into the new world, re-named as Br'er Rabbit, finally turned into a literary figure and then into a technicolor cartoon? Or do gods take pleasure in their storied transmutations? Is Trickster revitalized by even a Disney imagination—is it one of his tricks? More significantly for our time, what about the gods whose stories are forgotten completely except by students or pedants? What happens to the world if no one can tell the story of how Isis made her serpent with the spittle of Ra? Is the world thinned, faded, made more fragile?

Whatever we do in our lives, we make text of our lives. Whether or not our stories belong to the shared patterns of the great, true stories—the myths—they are the texts from which we find out our relation to the divine, to one another, and to the self.

Isis wearied of the myriads of humans and longed to join the myriads of gods. She noticed that Father Ra, growing old, drooled as he made his daily solar journey across his double kingdom. She waited surreptitiously until Ra went past, drooling in the pathway. She kneaded the spittle together with the dust of the earth and made—as children always do when they begin to work with clay—a snake. She placed her serpent in the way and the next time Ra came walking by, as he liked to survey his kingdom, the serpent of Isis bit him. He howled so that all the myriads of gods gathered. Isis asked one of the rhetorical questions famous on such occasions: "Oh, Father Ra, has a serpent bitten you?"

"Yes, my daughter, a serpent has bitten me and I am as cold as water and as hot as fire." (Even the illnesses of the gods are formed of paradox.) Isis, a witch, a healer, offered to cure him, "if you will tell me, Father, your secret name."

Ra began to recite his great names, his great attributes; he is the one who causes the Nile to flood, the crops to grow, the sun to make its journey, the bull to mount the cow. . . .

"Yes, we know all those names," Isis replied. "Tell me your secret, sacred name." Ra refused until the fire burned hotter, the water washed colder, and he became inarticulate.

Then he consented that Isis should know his secret name. They departed from the presence of the other gods and Ra permitted Isis to enter into him. She entered the body of Ra and learned and took the sacred name, becoming a goddess, the most compassionate goddess in the Near East in her caring for humanity.

What have we lost if we have lost that story? Certainly its components resonate with everything from the Garden of Eden to the Logos of the Gospel of John; but it creates and alters the universe in its own fashion. Perhaps if we lose the story of Isis, we lose a means by which the divine word can be tricked or stolen from the remote realm and come to reside within the maker, or compassionate goddess; that is, we lose one of the stories that can make the divine come to live within ourselves.

Isis became a goddess because she incorporated the divine name, gave body to text.

It seems that this particular ancient story of the fortunate treachery of Isis is expendable, can be forgotten; but the retelling of that story—the story of the making of text—cannot be lost. How is it that each of us performs the trick of capturing the divine word? It must be that since the stories never give away any secrets but their own narratives (the story of Isis tells us that she captured the divine word—it does not give the divine word except as the story itself), the making of story is the making of the universe. It must be that whatever we do, say, think, creates the universe. The stories we tell, even the ones we forget, might be called the making of sacred text. And text is giving shape to the universe.

⌒⌒

Long before writing was invented, human beings read their world. They interpreted their dreams and the flights of birds. They read the intestines of sacrificial animals and the memories of their ancestors. They read the things that surprised them, or the things that reminded them of something else. Most of all, they read in the places where there were holes—spaces—gaps. They filled up the blanks of the universe, as though they were pages, with writing. Leonardo advised aspiring artists to "discover" the pictures to be found in the cracks in walls; Chinese sages were conceived as their mothers stepped into the footprints of unicorns; all of us make up our lives out of the cracks in the walls of our past memories and the unicorn footprints of our futures. The making of a life is similar to the making of a text. We live by reading our own stories. We read by recall and imagination. A sacred text is made by making up what is felt to be already there, just like a life. A sacred text is an impression in stone, or imagination filling up the maker of the space.

Natural indentations in stones are credited with the impress of wonderful beings; they bear the memory of divine presence. An imprint, a cleft, is read as a holy text. The place where

there is nothing is perceived as the place where something was, and thus the place where meaning will locate itself. There is a stone footprint where the Buddha, the Christ, or Muhammad touched the earth—depending upon the vocabulary of its reader; Trickster's stone boiling pot and dish, from which he ate his last meal on earth, rest beside the stone that retains the impress of his buttocks, even of his testicles. Fraudulent dinosaur and human tracks walk together in order to tell a story outside history, attempting to verify a feeble text. There are dents that were made in rocks by the heads of saints at the moments of their forceful births. Yahweh wrote the Ten Commandments with his own finger on a stone, which Moses broke in an iconoclastic rage; God had to recopy his own work, redoing the tablets of the law so that they would be ultimately "written in the hearts" of his people. Sacred text is the palpable imprint of the divine, which can be traced over again, renewed and reimagined. Religion is the act of reading.

A sacred text is a means of divining one's inner self and one's relationship to the world of meaning. A sacred text reveals to us our own identity, interpreting our present and calling up our future all in terms of our past—in terms of the old story. We hear the lament that the Bible is a forgotten text, reduced to an idol by fundamentalists, used as apocalyptic decoder-map for some, as a book of etiquette for others. What has happened to the book as locus of sacrality? Childhood recall offers, "You couldn't set anything on top of the Bible or bad would come into the house"; yet those same persons are ignorant of the withering of the fig tree, Moses in the cleft of the rock, or even the sacrifice of Isaac.

Texts are not bodies of information but embodiments of interpretation. They are mythic, and contain as well the methods for demythologizing themselves. Text tells the secret of discrimination as well as conjunction, of separation as well as connection, of iconoclasm as well as myth-making. Text has been mistaken for an explanatory code for the exterior rather than as the revelation of the interior. Text functions to originate, focus, and enhance the interpretation of the self and the world. It tells lies in order to create truth. Our texts are like our boxes.

As boxes are borders around spaces, texts are words around silences.

Sacred objects, prototypical of the Ark of the Covenant, have been focal points in numerous Bedouin tribes. The "box" was often made of wooden poles, sometimes decorated with black ostrich plumes, always empty and guarded within the tribal chief's tent. Oaths were sworn on it, sacrificial blood was smeared on it, and when the tribe went to war, the ark was placed on a camel, leading the men into battle. Any of three presences might have been located within this emptiness. As the ark went into battle, a young, marriageable relative of the chief would sit within it, loosening her hair and garments, urging the warriors to defend the ark with their lives. Sometimes, as the Bedouin were converted to Islam, the Koran was suspended from the center within the ark. And it was said that when the plumes vibrated and the ark shifted when neither wind nor person had touched it, Allah himself had come to reside within it. In that nothingness then, only the feminine, the holy text, or the god could dwell. Around it all the ceremonies of life were clustered.[1]

The nature of text is not to be found merely in canonical documents but in the way we decipher and interpret reality. We have come to wonder how we will read sacrality in a culture derived from "people of the book" but amongst people who no longer, or can no longer, read. It may be that we are entering a period of the renewal of the word—of texting reality—for disintegration and regeneration are steps in the same dance. Our culture may find itself alienated from its textual tradition, but human beings are never "textless"—we cannot help making text, formulating our images into phrases, our dreams into lives.

ᥴᥱ

Illiterate, unpersuaded by and uninterested in the Holy Book his wife places on a crocheted doily by the stiffest chair, he is a man who nevertheless, whenever he wants to heighten his stories or strengthen his points, will say, "Now, son, it's in The

Book." The book is the text of his own life, the interweaving of his own experience and imagination.

Why does a man who cannot read claim, "It's in the book, son"? Why does someone who does not follow a faith that is tied to a particular text cite an imaginary one?

The easiest answer is that it is a common cliché used for emphasis; surely it has no more significance. The most reasonable answer is that it is simply a low-level participation in the dominant culture, which is presided over by a textual consciousness. Indeed, if we bend round back of the cliché and look for its source—the imaginative impulse that forms our clichés—and if we bend round back of the textuality of western culture to find the imaginative impulse that forms our reality, then we come to see that to say "it's in The Book" is to say that it participates in eternal truth, that it has authority, perhaps even that it can be verified (you can look it up). To say "it's in The Book" is to place oneself within its pages.

We live in a time, we are told, in which there is a literacy crisis and a disengagement from traditional religious texts, an emerging era of the postliterate, or nonlinear culture; but since we come from a text-oriented culture and religion, what form will the making of sacred text now take? It is the impulse that focuses our lives, and to demonstrate it, I have begun with the illiterate man, who never went through literacy and will never achieve the postliterate age. On the periphery of a biblical fundamentalism—textuality turned to mere literalism—he remythologizes The Book so that he can read it, not merely literally, but in the manner of sacred text.

From gossip to records of significant liminal experiences,[2] we are formulating the universe—writing sacred text. Little phrases, anecdotes, threads of family history become "text" when they are repeated, embroidered, given new contexts, and finally serve to interpret other events. Each family has its own stories, anecdotes, threads of histories, and wonderful lies, that are repeated and saturated with the lives of those who hold them in their memories. As those childhood "boxes" can reveal something of the impulse for finding the sacred in ordinary experience, so can the casual tale, family anecdote, or even the joke, uncover something of the rudimentary form, the radical metaphorical impulse for making experience into text.

There is another figure on the peripheries of literacy, who eloquently speaks of textuality. "One time many years ago," a Blackfeet reported around the turn of the century, "I had been sick for so long a time I expected to die."

A sweathouse was made and prayers were said for him; he went up on a hill and ". . . prayed to everything I could see for help." Returning to his tipi he slept and "In my sleep help came to me."

He dreamed an old man came and demanded, "Give me the letter."

The dreamer said he had no letter, nothing upon which there was writing.

The old man repeated, "Yes, you have a letter and I want it."

The dreamer insisted he had no letter.

"Yes, you have a letter," said the old man, and reaching into the dreamer's belly pulled out a letter. "This is what made you sick," he said, "now you will get well."

The dreamer glimpsed the letter, which he said resembled a piece of glass with writing on one side. And the dreamer recovered and became a medicine man.[3]

Text is that which resides in the belly like a piece of glass, tormenting one nearly to death; and text is the dream which wrenches the glass shard from the belly, healing.

Reality can be discovered only by reading it; most of humanity has at some time or another deciphered the texts of animal footprints, the sound of water, the lines in the palms of their hands, the constellations, the arrangements of stones. Whatever we perceive religiously we "read"; that is, we interpret— we find meaning in relation to ourselves. The external is internalized.

Not long ago I was hurrying to improvise a potluck dish. As I layered the ingredients into tortillas, folding them into packets, lining them up in the pan, my cheese ran low. Rather than grate more cheese, I began to skimp, sprinkling rather than heaping the cheese. I suddenly heard my father's voice, "Heap up and shake down and the Lord'll bless you." Where did the phrase emerge from? Several times when I was a child, my father told a story about when he was a boy that always amused him but was senseless to me.

He had been hired by an old lady to harvest apples from her tree. He was careless; the apples barely covered the bottom of the bushel basket. The lady came outside and said to him, "Now, honey, heap up and shake down and the Lord'll bless you."

He shook the tree, gathered the apples, more than filled the basket, and collected his nickel. Something in the woman's remark amused him so profoundly that he occasionally would tell the anecdote and chuckle. I didn't think it was funny or meaningful. Yet years later the line came back to rebuke me in a moment of haste and carelessness. The old woman, no doubt, believed in a simple pay-as-you-go-with-virtue form of religious morality, but my father does not. He kept the phrase, not because he believes in the pay-in-service-obtain-a-reward form of pseudo-religion, but because the way one does something "texts" who one is. I remembered—by the reverberation of a story that had never interested me—that making dinner makes a self. The layering of cheese, just as animal footprints for the ancients, is a text.

Each family has phrases, often composed of decomposed jokes or composite fragments of memory, which have the quality of text. The anecdotes are repeated or the moments reconstructed until they are part of the listeners' being. Some sacred texts have no more noble origins. "This is the tree that your grandmother planted and watered every day when she emptied the tub," is the mundane correspondent to the date palm that Deborah sat beneath or the tamarisk that Abraham planted. The old man who shouted in his Irish brogue over the tenor's voice at the funeral of his longtime good friend, "Be quiet, now, or you'll be waking the old bat up," made a fuss at the funeral, but made a text for his great-grandchildren.

In a secular world that has lost its ritualistic or textual orientation to reality, stories, both the ancient ones and the contemporary, personal ones, become more essential to create a reality that binds us to the divine as it loosens us from our limitations. There is a story recounted by Gershom Scholem that tells us about the nature of story itself:

> When the Baal Shem had a difficult task before him, he would go to a certain place in the woods, light a fire and meditate in prayer—and what he had set out to perform was done. When a generation later the Maggid of Messeritz was faced with the same task he would go to the same place in the woods and say: We can no longer light the fire, but we can still speak the prayers—and what he wanted became reality. Again a generation later Rabbi Moshe Leib of Sassov had to perform this task. And he too went into the woods and said: We can no longer light a fire, nor do we know the secret meditations belonging to the prayer, but we do know the place in the woods to which it all belongs—and that must be sufficient; and sufficient it was. But when another generation had passed and Rabbi Israel of Rishin was called upon to perform the task, he sat down on his golden chair in his castle and said: We cannot light the fire, we cannot speak the prayers, we do not know the place, but we can tell the story of how it was done. And, the storyteller adds, the story which he told had the same effect as the actions of the other three.

We may lose—as we have—the ritual, the sacred place, the holy words, but the power of "text" persists through memory and imagination, through telling the story. *Text*, etymologically, refers to weaving; and it is the weaving of imagination and discovery, of the divine and the human, of the past and the present, that creates the fabric of our existence. We all have bits and scraps of experience, dream, and thought out of which we weave the texture, the story, of our lives. The metaphors within which we reside link us to the symbolic quality of the divine.

Secular history tricks us into believing that we are completely demythologized or lost to story, that because we cannot light the fire, speak the prayers, know the place, we cannot remember (or make up) the story. Secular history itself is a making up (or remembering) of the story. It is a familiar tale, similar to its sacred displacement. Secular history resembles those myths in which the gods depart, withdraw, become obscure. Sky God once lay very close to Mother Earth, but the people let smoke from their cooking fires sting his eyes; they reached above their heads to dry their hands, using God for a towel; and one old woman even cut off little pieces of him to enhance her stew. So Sky God withdrew, far away; now human beings cannot reach him. Our "secularization" process might be characterized as the withdrawal of the divine from the world;[4] secular history is another form of the myth of sacred departure.

There is nothing to recover; it is only a question of rediscovering what lies inherent in these profound texts. Whenever the crisis of divine departure or obscurity weighs upon the human, someone invents a metaphor—makes a connection. Lao Tzu looked at the way water seeks the lowest level, called it feminine and declared it humble; yet, he said, it wears away the hardest stone. He said that the great force of water is gentle, almost like nothing. Lao Tzu said that it takes thirty spokes to make a wheel, but the usefulness of the wheel depends upon the place where there is nothing; we use clay to make a vessel, turning it round, but the usefulness of the vessel depends upon the place where there is nothing; we make a house by piercing doors and windows in the structure, for it is in the place where there is nothing that the usefulness of the house resides. Lao Tzu made his metaphor of "nothing." Muhammad heard the Angel Gabriel tell him that humans were created from blood and taught by the pen. Thus, Muhammad said, "The ink of the scholar is holier than the blood of martyrs," and text and life are connected by that metaphor of blood and ink. Uddalaka instructed his son, Svetaketu, in the *Chandogya Upanishad,* to open up a fig. The son found little seeds. Open one of the seeds, said his father. The son found what his father wanted him to discover, the "essence" that looks like "nothing." Through the layers of *maya* one will come to the metaphor of the divine. One would resist conflating the hazelnut experience of Julian of Norwich, the ink (word) which transcends blood in the Koran, Lao Tzu's spaces and places generating the ten thousand things, the peeling away of the layers by Svetaketu, because that process would take away the stories, the particular metaphorical means that each of these traditions has found to rediscover the sacred. One would resist, too, I think, forcing our contemporary experiences of making boxes, texts, jokes, plays, into "sacred" forms. The resistance to codifying these is part of their sacred quality, the means to telling the story, repeating the joke.

Memory makes text, and so does its opposite, the joke. Most often we think of the joke as the maligner or deflater of religion. Parodies have followed religious rituals, it seems, for as long as there have been such ceremonies. Sometimes the mockery has not played so much at destroying the religious ritual as it has extended and embroidered, or re-imagined, the sacred. Indeed, surprise as much as recall awakens the sense of the sacred in our lives. Moses was astonished by the paradoxical burning bush, Muhammad by the angel, Siddhartha by the four passing sights. But sometimes the surprise edges upon the joke. When Sarah heard that she would at last give birth to a child in her old age, she laughed. The child was named "laughter" or Isaac.

A three-year-old child helping her mother cook saw a carton put back into the cupboard and exclaimed, "Wait. Stop. Look at that! It keeps going back!" It was her first encounter with an image of infinity, the box that featured a picture of itself in which there was a picture of itself, etc. That simple illustration so delighted the child that it moved her by amusement into an expanded vision of reality. The comic, when spontaneously encountered, expands into the cosmic. Words become worlds, laughter becomes the creative force of the universe.

The Zen tradition is laced together with the profundity of laughter. In Zen the Buddha was silent, regardless of the volumes of scriptures attributed to him; he taught by pointing. Seeming commonplaces offer the possibility that they may explode into the deepest mystery. The old Zen question "How do you get a live goose out of a bottle?" is much like its counterpart "If all is reduced to the One—to what is the One reduced?" offering the possibility that the goose is out.

The moments that amuse us are close to the moments that amaze us. Those little occasions, as when a child turns our thinking with a silly phrase like "bird breath," are at the lower

end of a continuum with the "beautiful naked boy" of Meister
Eckhart.

> Meister Eckhart met a beautiful naked boy.
> He asked him where he came from.
> He said: "I come from God."
> Where did you leave him?
> "In virtuous hearts."
> Where are you going?
> "To God."
> Where do you find him?
> "Where I part from all creatures."
> Who are you?
> "A king."
> Where is your kingdom?
> "In my heart."
> Take care that no one divide it with you!
> "I shall."
> Then he led him to his cell.
> Take whichever coat you will.
> "Then I should be no king!"
> And he disappeared.
> For it was God himself—
> Who was having a bit of fun.[5]

God has fun, says the Eckhart legend; the universe was created from the Hindu principle of *lila*, the play of Brahman; or,
as the folk tradition claims, the child Jesus made clay birds just
as the other children did, but touched his and made them fly.
But this element of religious consciousness is most often missing from dualistic systems. Play belongs to the "other" (as Wes-
ley said, "It's a pity the devil has all the best tunes"); dualists
have to be serious. Play, however, is that which creates image
and idea, which makes metaphor.

ᝃᝅ

Among required transgressions—like stealing an apple,
eavesdropping, touching a snake—is trespassing the cemetery;
as soon as the bike can make it up Pete's Hill, and the absence

can be accounted for (*"Where were you?"*), the ride of passage is committed.

This year, I didn't even realize, it was my daughter's turn. I thought she would stay closer; the sudden nest under the eave, easily spied from the window—wasn't that mystery enough for this time? To see the scrawny mouth turn to fat, blinking ball, and then to bird flying—wasn't that enough for this summer? I'm still undone by it.

But today she said, "Are you allowed to talk by graves?"

"Yes," I said.

So she decided to talk to me. "I went to the cemetery. There were old ladies there. One was talking to a grave; she said, 'Bless your heart.'" The girl is getting old, teetering on the edge of this nest, contemptuous of easy words, pieties pinned so often to her cheek and curl; today she saw those easy words poured out on a grave.

"And did you talk?" I asked.

She did, but didn't now.

Coming back round, she complained, "You can't find anyone there. It's such a stupid graveyard. They are not even in alphabetical order."

"Who?"

"The graves."

"People don't die in alphabetical order," I laughed, unconcealing the great chaos.

"How are you supposed to find anybody?"

"Who were you looking for?"

"We looked for Katie's brother. They should have them in alphabetical order if they expect you to find anybody."

The brother, born too soon and never breathing, was he there?

And, returning once more, she asked, "How do you like the name Anna Eliza?"

"Yes. Who is it?"

"Anna Eliza Harper. She's one of the graves. I thought you'd like her name," she said, meaning she did.

One of the old graves, I thought; a stone lamb she will not reveal. Did she speak to Anna Eliza? Did she quicken a ghost?

Did she lie down and under, beside her? Would she file her under H or A or L for lamb? Can she find secrets in the alphabet? How did she learn that cemeteries are for reading?

And later, the dog, fat and clumsy (no one thought he could), grabbed a young bird in the grass. Everyone screamed and scolded, echoing the mother robin's cry and flutter. The dog, enlivened by the taste of motion, and unashamed, was banished, smiling, to the house.

"It's alive. It'll be all right," pronounced my daughter to my surprise, the one who had just visited with death.

In the house, she put her arms around the dog and comforted the villain. "You didn't know, did you? You dear," she crooned. "You can't help it. You don't know what you're doing. It's not your fault."

She saw me looking, and putting her face next to the dog's, said, "You dear Bird Breath," and muffled her laugh in his ruff.

She, I knew then, had learned some alphabet in the cemetery that day; and this season had come too soon for me, when my daughter has begun to read the letters carved on my mortality. And Anna Eliza, "bless your heart," I must talk with you.

3

Personal Events and Cultural Dreams Memory and Imagination

Carmen Miranda, dancer of a previous generation, emerged one evening in pale memories roused by the caricature Chiquita Banana. A curious child, inspired by ruffled skirts and hats filled with fruits, began the next day to draw a picture of Carmen Miranda dancing, with fruits on her head, fruits falling, fruits on the floor. The fallen fruits were quarreling with the dancer: "Watch your step, Carmen!" and "Don't dance on me!" they shouted in cartoon balloons.

Memories, removed by two generations, are acts of imagination. The story heard and told is a new creation. The event serves as impetus for memory; and recall makes a new story, gradually spinning itself into its transformed existence. Who would have thought that Carmen Miranda could be spun through three generations? Or who would have suspected that the story of Balaam's ass in the Book of Numbers could have been preserved, canonized, and revitalized for so many ongoing generations?

Memory may be formed of two sources or two forces colliding: an experience in the present which evokes and collides with a sensation or an awareness of the past. Memories might be considered artistic inventions, that is, as the work of metaphor: repetition, mingling, or juxtaposition.

They may be formed of *repetition* as when two similar images resonate, the former shadowing the present. Children used to visit a house in their neighborhood just to have a look at the bronzed high-heeled shoes that graced the mantel. They had been the favorite shoes of a deceased wife, enshrined by the husband and regularly dusted by the second wife. Someone placed a pair of high-heeled shoes on a shelf, spontaneously recalling the vision of the bronzed shoes and creating, in the simple act of putting shoes on a shelf, a grotesque emblem of death, of a *memento mori*. Memory, as intended here, is not simply the recall of the bronzed shoes, but is the recall of the attraction of the children toward their experience of the bizarre, when by means of a repetition of image, shoes on a shelf, a new complex is created. Memory is an imaginal constellation of past and present that generates a new experience. Memory is not the storing of the past, but the storying of the present.

Or memory may be made of *mingling,* as when parts of one join with aspects of a second. It is as dependent upon the elements forgotten or upon what has been left out, as upon the tension that brings the disparate into accord. The sound of a word, the precision of an act, creates a world, an art, a semblance of the ordinary that replicates the perfect. Religious experience makes memory palpable; when memory takes over, ordinary time is dispelled. In religious terms, one enters the eternal, in poetic terms, the metaphor. If the story of Moses is recalled, we will be religious wanderers; if the story of David is evoked, we will dwell in a holy kingdom. Whatever we remember we construct. As events are recalled over the years, time colors them, rearranges them. Not that the memory is faulty, but rather the memory is nimble, innovative, interpretative. Memory works in more than one direction, according to the classic statement on the subject, Lewis Carroll's *Through the Looking Glass,* where the Queen tries to influence Alice into becoming her servant with the offer of "jam every other day."

"It's very good jam," said the Queen.

"Well, I don't want any *to-day,* at any rate."

"You couldn't have it if you *did* want it," the Queen said. "The rule is, jam to-morrow and jam yesterday—but never jam *to-day.*"

"It *must* come sometimes to 'jam to-day,' " Alice objected.

"No, it ca'n't," said the Queen. "It's jam every *other* day: and to-day isn't any other day, you know."

"I don't understand you," said Alice.

"It's the effect of living backwards," the Queen said kindly: "it always makes one a little giddy at first—"

"Living backwards!" Alice repeated in great astonishment. "I never heard of such a thing!"

"—but there's one great advantage in it, that one's memory works both ways."

"I'm sure *mine* only works one way," Alice remarked. "I ca'n't remember things before they happen."

"It's a poor sort of memory that only works backwards," the Queen remarked.

"What sort of things do *you* remember best?" Alice ventured to ask.

"Oh, things that happened the week after next," the Queen replied in a careless tone.[1]

The joke is finally on any reader who fails to realize that memory is a tangle rather than a single taut thread. Memory mingles one experience with another.

Scholarly quarrels abound over whether various great religious thinkers should be in the category of innovator or reformer—whether they were remembering forward or backward. Whatever a religious experience is, it is the mingling of memory, the creation of story. A six-year-old girl one day picnicked upon cantaloupe with her friend, who presented her with an old compact. It was a fine treasure, discarded by the boy's mother, with compartments, mirrors, and bits of makeup under the little doors. The child—or rather, the woman recalling that event—claimed to have experienced a strange sensation when her boyfriend from across the street gave her the wonderful compact. She said she suddenly thought, "This reminds me of some time when a wonderful man will give me a beautiful compact." The past event and the forward memory resided undisturbed for years until, she said, "The only ten dollars we had was frivolously spent on an antique compact embossed with fairies." It was as though the childhood event were a memory turned inside-out of the "box" experience of her mature love.

Or memory may be formed of a curious *juxtaposition* of two seemingly disparate images joined by a motive in a person's mind. Alice in Wonderland can come to reside with Jacob and his ladder of angels; or the scent of watermelon can join with the sound of Bach. Memory often is made up as much of fantasy as of recovered information. Memory makes stories of the past by giving shape to fragments of lost experience, and stories the present by giving depth to the immediate.

The Greeks claimed the mother of all the muses is Mnemosyne, Memory. It is Memory who *mythologically* gives birth to the arts; she is the dominant disguise of Imagination. There is a story that suggests that the power of recall may not have as much to do with recapturing the past as with inventing the present:

ᆺᄀ

It was hot. She told herself that the air was pulsating like a disembodied dragon's heart pumping dead heat. She was fond of thinking such things. Yet, it was an ordinary day. She thought the leaves in the trees rattled like myriads of tiny bells that had swallowed their clappers and choked on the sounds of their rings. It was an ordinary time nevertheless. She told herself that the air was remembering something that had already happened.

There was a large sharp stone in her left shoe. She kept walking, feeling the stone, trying to see it with her foot. It was unusually large and sharp, but it is an ordinary thing to get a stone in the shoe.

If she were more like an oyster, she wished, she could wrap a luminous thread round and round the stone and turn it into a big, baroque pearl by the time she got home. But with this wish she could thread only the pain, not the stone. So she curved round and round the little pains in her foot until she at last sat down on the rough boards of her own back porch, screened by pea vines and morning glories, and unbuckled her shoe. She spilled the stone into her palm and then into her lap. It was a brilliant, enormous, faceted diamond, lost into its freedom from a defective setting and a hapless engagement. She looked at it and remembered how she had tried to wind it into a mere pearl. But there was nothing unusual about the moment; it was an ordinary irony even if it was an unusual stone.

The next day was hot. She said to herself that the air churned as though she were caught in the midst of an invisible battle with unseen swords and stones whirling past her. It was an unusual time. She said aloud that the leaves in the trees rattled like someone was trying to choke life out of dry skeletons. It was an extraordinary day. She could not remember another day like it.

She built a little booth, like a child's lemonade stand, and printed DIAMOND FOR TRADE in black letters. She sat in her booth waiting for offers. MAKE ME AN OFFER, she amended to her stand when it was almost noon.

She wished she were a princess so that she would not have been obliged to discover the diamond in her shoe and set up her diamond-for-trade stand. She didn't know any stories that told her what to expect in her own circumstances. If she were a princess, people would make her offers anyway, no trades. But with this wish she could only imagine the offers made to a princess; she could not imagine being a princess.

At last they came, forming a line that went around the bend in the road. The first man offered to make her a princess. It was an ordinary offer but an unusual irony. She passed him on.

All that day she received offers of marriage, offers of islands, of cottages and castles; she was offered a part with a traveling road show; she was offered a tame bear who wore a little tassled jacket. They came and proposed adventures sexual and spiritual. One man proposed to take over and run the diamond-for-trade stand; it was her most unusual offer.

She grew tired and wished God himself would come and make her an offer, but it was only an unusual day in an ordinary story. God wished not to appear in it.

The last man offered her a book with a brass clasp, filled with loose pages of unusual stories. "I usually make them up myself," she said, but traded the diamond for the book.

The man stayed on; they had adventures sexual and spiritual; they got rich and bought a pet bear and acted with him in a road show. He was an unusual man; the book was rare; but the stories they read and lived were the ones to be expected after finding a diamond in a shoe. It was as though the stories were enormous diamonds when they read them, but like large, baroque pearls when they lived them.

The man had been engaged before, but wouldn't tell that story. He claimed amnesia. She wondered if the diamond held by his own memory, if it was from his former engagement. So to get back at him she pretended he was God, or forgot how she met him, or mixed up the stories. It was an ordinary marriage but an unusual love.

ᔑᓄ

Parables are not allegories; they offer no maps but shift false maps into alternate universes. Stories will not tell us how memory works, but stories remembered may be parables of memory itself. The stories we remember are the narratives that interpret our own lives, whether they are from the traditional narrative arts or from our own fragments of our pasts.

How will we be able to remember what is important rather than helplessly recall the capricious distractions of odds and ends pulled from memory's messy handbag? Medieval and Renaissance minds developed a complete Art of Memory to preserve their elusive truths. The Art of Memory was dependent upon the assumption that we might remember better the lies we invent than the truths we are given, that the necessary might slip from us unless attached to the frivolous. However, in the metaphorical sense, the frivolous can be another form of truth. The images serve not only to remind us of the contents, but to participate in the meaning of the contents, adding a dimension of depth and mystery.

Personal memories make up the stuff of our lives; when people are dying they need to recapitulate themselves, cast themselves into an art form, a story, for whoever will pause to listen, to listen and to re-member them. People who are changing, emerging, "getting born" also cast themselves into story. Inevitably these stories or mythologies of ordinary lives are littered, just like the great sacred stories, with stones, jokes, miracles, lies, bones, animals, and angels.

Memory is made up of imagination and creates the presence that we dwell in. Private memories are like sacred texts. Sacred text creates a cultural universe; memory creates a microcosmic one. To recapture the past is to understand the self symbolically.

❧

Very first memories of individuals recapitulate the great myths of our civilization.

A few very first memories are imagistic or tactile impressions involving little more than form and texture; it may be the imprint of the quilt someone sat on and crawled on (before walking upright and before falling). Another tells us, "I remember being held in my mother's arms. There was a black lace inset in her black dress that looped around her neck. She must have had that dress for years because later I called it her finger dress or her snake dress. The designs looked like fingers or snakes to me. I didn't like the dress; but I can still feel how soft my mother was."

Most first memories are more dramatic. Over and over again, they illustrate a single story. At any random gathering of people, the collection of "first memories" produces curious and profound correspondences. For example, from one such group: "I was sitting in my stroller and a whole bowl of cherries was put in my lap." / "My baby sister was brought home from the hospital. I wasn't supposed to touch her. She looked different from me and my parents acted different." / "I had to go to kindergarten. I didn't want to go. My mother took me there and left me." / "My father died on the way home, coming across the field. Someone picked me up and said, 'Don't cry, he saved something special for you in his lunchbox.'" / "I took a drink of coffee. I wasn't allowed to have any. It tasted terrible." / "My dad went to get some things at the bakery and slammed the car door on my fingers." / "I fell out of my crib." / "I always rode 'horse' on my Grandpa's leg; one time he bucked me off and I fell down." / "I went running up to a dog and it bit me." / "My mother was lying on the bed and I was bouncing on her. She said, 'Don't jump. Be careful now. There's a baby in there.' "

These fragments of image and feeling resonate in a larger design. That design is our collective "first memory," the story of the Fall in the biblical tradition. These first memories (whether accurate recall or imagination) together make up something like the great cultural story of the Fall: First there is Paradise, Eden, perfect and confined like a baby's multicolored quilt or being held by mother, a protected place. Even in Paradise, in mother's arms, there is a disturbing glimpse—like fingers or snakes in the lace of her dress, the serpent in the greenery. Thrust into that perfection comes the temptation—what may seem like a fruit, a "bowl of cherries" but is bitter as that first forbidden taste of coffee; reaching toward the bakery our fingers are slammed in the car door by Father. Grandpa Himself lets us or causes us to Fall, and pleasure becomes concurrent with pain. Something new enters the world, but the dog bites, the new baby makes everyone act strangely, and we are thrown out of the Garden, left by mother at the kinder-Garden; death enters the world—but death with the promise of "something saved" in the lunchbox. Human pain enters, but so does promise.

These particular memories parallel or echo an archaic story because they, like the archaic narrative, evoke an imaginative beginning. The individual first memory, like the cultural first story, is the fall into self-consciousness. From the fall, the conclusion, comes the origin, the waking.

My grandmother's first memory, she has told us, is about the mean midwife named Mary who came to stay at their house when my grandmother's little brother was born. The midwife supplied the story, as everything from the Vedas to Plato have supplied it, of where we came from, the primeval story of creation. "I found him by the spring when I went to get water," said Mary. "He was playing and skipping around the creek."

"Then why can't he walk now?" asked the child.

"Because I had to break his legs so he wouldn't run away."
(It's called an *etiology*, part of all origins stories, telling why it is
that serpents crawl on their bellies, or why new babies can't
walk.)

The little girl feared the midwife, rubbed her little brother's
legs, and years later remembered the story, remembered her
fear of Mary, the feel of her baby brother's little legs, and her
first encounter with the great questions—the stuff from which
religious consciousness might be forged.

Memory is fundamental to religion; and religion might be
defined as the repository of, and the means to conjure up, the
essential memories of the human mind. Religious institutions
contain and shape the universe by remembering the creation,
by remembering what it means to be human. The great western traditions, indeed, gave memory its most prominent religious function by coming to understand reality through the
concept of sacred history.

Sacred history informed "the people of the book" that their
present was manufactured from the impress of the past, and
that their future was already shaped by it. What was unique
was the expression and celebration of a coherent cultural and
metaphysical memory. Put another way, the following story or
parable of memory places the unique in the context of repetition; as memory itself is a repetition of the unique, this music
we play of ourselves, inventing harmonies out of the chaos of
our thoughts and lives.

ↄ

Twice or three times it had happened; and each time it
occurred as though original, unique, and ignorant of prece-
dent or subsequent. When it was about to happen again, however, the prior models were stumbled upon; and though they
were not recognized, they effected a change.

*

The first time, it may have been the first, a man named
John, wearing an animal-skin shirt, turned toward Mary his
wife. She was wearing a blue gown she had colored herself
from berries. The stain held more tenaciously to her hands

than to the cloth. "I can't get it out of my hands and I can't get it to stay in the cloth."

"Mary," he said, "I have a dream that does not leave me. So I must leave here."

Mary, who had neither word nor concept for map, looked at the dark-dyed lines in her hands and imagined them as the furrows of her garden, recalling the parsley next to the onions. But then she saw those stains as the roads John would walk and the rivers he would have to wade. She feared the places her palm took her, on to the home of the bloody Saracens, and back to the walls of Eden. Then she saw, under her second and third fingers, inked stars; and she saw that the roads in her hand circumscribed God's whole universe. She turned to John, but he had already gone.

*

The second, or maybe the third time it happened, a woman named Miriam turned toward her husband, Joseph, just as he held up his spoon between them and remarked, as he often did to her, "How is it, Miriam, that the spoon becomes bent into a shape contrary to its function? The silver becomes fatigued and the bowl moves to an angle counter to the stem; the result is that the spoon is so cumbersome, the pudding falls from it and stains my clothes. Or I take the pudding so quick, it burns my tongue."

Miriam waited until he completed his recurring complaint and then said, "Joseph, I have had a dream that does not leave me; so I must return to it. I'm going to my bed, and I won't get up again."

Joseph, bowed toward the pudding traces on his coat, felt his wounded tongue against his teeth, and wondered if the food was making a violent attack against him. Pelting his chest, stinging his tongue, it acted out a penultimate reminder that the pudding was not yet Joseph. But when the pudding becomes me, he thought, and I turn it into my work and my talk, will it remember how it was coaxed into its previous state by Miriam at the oven? And will it, then I, know Miriam? Turning toward Miriam, no longer beside him, he saw she had already departed.

*

Now the time we come to, the time of deviation, when the scene was about to be recapitulated and with all the feeling of a first time which is necessary to a repetition, there was a man named James. He turned toward his wife, Mecret, just as she turned toward him. They were climbing a hillside; and as they both began to speak at once, causing a shudder to Mecret's rhythm, she fell against the stones, cutting her arm, rushing the deep red to the opened surface. They stopped then, when they came to the next level, and seated against an ancient evergreen, their legs extending only to the first joint of its roots, Mecret turned again toward James as he turned toward her.

She gave him the stone she'd been carrying for him, a rough gray slab, indented with the memory of a sea shell. He ran his finger over the ridges of a primal world.

"I have a stone for you," he said; but she was watching her blood. He took her arm and placed the sliced skin against her knee. She pulled it away and the grass stains on his pants met the blood from her arm.

"Show me," she said. It was a gray chunk, uniform in color, dull in shape. Then she turned it over, looking for a shell print and finding a tiny chamber nesting brilliant crystals.

"I must tell you, Mecret," James began, "that I have had a dream that does not leave me."

She stuck her tongue into the almond-shaped crystal cave and then said, "I have not left my bed for years, so that I would wander with you in this dream."

"This is not the dream," he said. "It's not an ordinary dream I speak of, as of one who colors her hands, or of another who soils his coat."

"We all have those dreams," sighed Mecret.

"This is another. It is forming itself, exuding itself into reality."

"Like a shell, or a crystal," she murmured. "Why don't you let the dream become one of those?"

"I don't want to hold it in my hand; it carries me."

"You recognize only the single chamber of the dream, the place where you dwell in it."

"Dreams cannot be seen from the outside."

Mecret took off her shirt, wrapped it, blue and green, round her arm, and started up the hill.

James followed, disappointed in her. Because she fell again, they took another way down, into a crevice of forest, and found a house made of four walls, rotted roof and earth floor.

"No bears, no ghosts," decided James.

"No treasure. No letters," added Mecret. "Why did we find this house if it holds no meaning?"

"It's like a house in a dream, but after you wake up," James said.

*

It was after that time, and the next time it happened, it must have been the third or fourth time, that Jules and Molly returned to the pursuit and loneliness of former times.

Their repetition was done as for the first time. Molly left Jules, for a dream she said, a dream that would not leave her.

Jules considered the bird's egg, broken on the rock. The interior of the shell was still moist; he turned to look at it and Molly turned away.

༺྅༻

In Plato's *Meno,* Socrates includes memory among the virtues of the soul and unravels his wonderful paradox of learning. Socrates draws a square in the dust and questions Meno's slave boy, demonstrating through his simple geometry lesson that we learn what we already know. Knowledge is not acquired, but remembered. "And if the truth of all things always existed in the soul, then the soul is immortal. Wherefore be of good cheer and try to recollect what you do not know, or rather what you do not remember."[2]

Cognition is recognition; thinking is the act of recall, and ignorance is not knowing how to ask the proper questions. "Without anyone teaching him, will he recover his knowledge for himself, if he is only asked questions?" Socrates asks, slyly pushing his dialogue partner into "remembering" that learning is a spontaneous recovery, or recollection, of inherent knowledge.

Religions generally have made a similar claim, that one must recover the inherent but dormant knowledge of truth. In a time when memory doesn't work all the way into eternity, meaning will nevertheless be made, and made of memory, fabricated of story. To lose the "eternal verities" means simply that one makes them up out of whatever is available, anything, perhaps as this parable might suggest:

༺༻

Once there was a girl, shy and pale, with Jean Harlow hair and glasses that made thin, gold circles around her eyes. She always did what she was told, never even scratching when her blue wool school uniform made her feel itchy. She got A's in Latin, English, and Math. She listened to the nuns on matters moral, intellectual, and practical. Only now and then metallic giggles would scrape from behind her hand.

Early in the fall, Sister demanded a short story. The girl, who was accustomed to populating her loneliness with figures formed from her pencil, worked and plotted and revised, trying rough scenes on the amateur stage of her imagination. She brought the story to English class. It was a lurid mystery. Sister took it to bed; after saying her beads she read it over twice again.

In mid-winter the girl transgressed. Hiding in the basement she secretly watched one of the nuns remove her habit. Out from under the voluminous black, the nun revealed her underwear. It was homemade and sturdy, constructed from available discarded fabric; and it was green. The girl's sharp giggle escaped from between her fingers when she saw the nun standing in the basement in green underwear. The nun looked toward the shadows and asked, "What did you expect?" No one told; there was no punishment.

Months went by, and one day Sister stopped the girl after English class. With a magazine rolled up and pressed against her crucifix, the nun said, "I didn't think they'd publish it. I didn't think they'd want it." Pleading and threatening, she handed the magazine to the girl. There was a story "by Sister Joseph Veronica," a lurid mystery, the words familiar. The girl looked through the magazine, saw her story in print along with pictures of beautiful ladies, gas stoves, home remedies, all garlanded with patriotic flags and eagles. She squinted her eyes behind her glasses and saw the name change to her own and then back to the nun's. "I don't care," she murmured, and gave back the magazine.

The girl continued to get A's and never went back to the basement. She developed a new interest in religion class. She studied the Doctrine of the Virgin Birth and felt that Joseph was being cheated out of his story. She studied the lives of the female saints who did astonishing things, cutting themselves out of dragon bellies, confounding pagan fathers and emperors with their quick tongues and Christian wisdom, and one who had wiped the sweating brow of Christ with a cloth that forever carried the imprint of the true image of the Lord.

Father thought that she was getting off the track; her interest in religion seemed to have passion, but no humility or devotion.

The next year, however, she became pregnant, married the young man in uniform, and almost forgot about it all. Sister was disappointed in her, said prayers for her, but soon almost forgot about her, too.

Years later, the girl turned woman told her daughter the story about how her mystery had been taken from her. Her daughter wrote it all down, stole the story of the nun's stealing, claiming to feel forever the imprint of the event as if she were a cloth into which her mother pressed her memories.

⌒

Memory is at work creating even the slightest and slenderest of a presence, out of pasts false or faded. Memory, or story, is the dressing up of the invisible, masquerading of the ineffable.

In the tenth canto of the *Inferno* Dante discovers that the damned remember the past and can see dimly into the future, "But when these things draw near, or when they are," they are unknown, hidden. The souls cannot understand or see the present; they are damned to past and future, never-never places that emphasize the semi-reality of damnation. They can only await the time in which they will look forward and see nothing: "When time's last hour shall shut the future's gate." The final prophecy is sightless silence. Dante's great poem is a geometrical construction strung upon memory and imagination. It looks to past and future, but does so in order to realize the present—to live in total present experience, that is, to achieve the state of the blessed. In *Purgatory*, souls can wash in the river Lethe,

the river of oblivion, to forget (purge) their sins. Dante and Virgil move against the stream as they leave Hell and travel toward recollection. Canto XX of *Inferno* shows the Sorcerers with heads twisted backward as punishment for trying to see ahead.

Perfect memory is an emblem of immortality; only the gods are beyond forgetting. The gods perform the primary task of creating the temporal out of the eternal, of remembering being. In traditional cultures old people are respected because they can remember—they can perform the holy task of linking the culture back upon itself. Perhaps one of the functions of love is for the lover to perform the intimate task of wrapping another within the chamber of memory, to carry and feel the love. In many religious structures the soul or self performs the ultimate task of remembering (re-creating) the potential self from the depth of its own being. Memory, then, whether the task of the gods that gives birth to the universe, the task of the old ones giving birth to culture, the task of lovers giving birth to the relational, or the task of the soul giving birth to being, must be reflections of the same task. That is why our religions and our lives are made up of these imperfect memories, the arts of our lives.

Memory keeps us awake at night, distracts us when we are working, hides when called upon, and tells us, over and over, that the consequence of memory's gift is the knowledge of death. Evocation of past carries inevitably a foretaste of future. As the past permits us to undo a little the deaths that have preceded us, so too it throws up a mirror before our own forgetting, which we call death.

4

The First Act Repeated
Myth and Contemporary
Consciousness

Recently I found myself confronted with a request to deliver a "Christmas" talk to a group of secularized, rational-humanist Unitarians, who did not presume or assume traditional modes yet desired something special for Christmas. Following my initial amusement at our inability not to practice what we will not preach, I decided to make as holy a spectacle as I could. Much rhetoric called for a little drama. So, I gathered up ten children and set about to assist them in creating and improvising their own "Christmas" play, curious about what children from non-traditionalist families with seemingly schizophrenic attitudes toward holy days would devise. Secularism, I suspect, is a pretense; at the very least it is an artificial attempt to dualistically divide a holistic world. Institutions, humanistic or not, are sometimes sarcophagi, petrified flesh eaters, hiding from us the religious character of experience. But religion is made of stories, of myths and dreams, which seep out of institutions and animate whatever their breath brushes. One of those authentic stories, a myth, was born in my presence in the humble straw of a Christmas play.

55

Myth cannot be defined by its archaic usages or by its exterior, formal qualities. That is, myth is not to be defined as a script for ritual or as stories about the gods. We can define myth only as the great story falling between drama and dream, a psychological structuring of the depth imagination. If we attempt to understand myth in sociological terms, or as a formation of corporate consciousness, then myth would be difficult to apprehend in this fragmented culture. But if myth is understood as carrying a psychological/aesthetic function, as the means of binding together fragmented experience and of giving reality or form to culture, then myth will indeed be apprehended in contemporary manifestations of the eternal imagination.

Myth is the narrative of depth that traces its vertical story on horizontal events. It may emerge as an individual's encounter with "soul" is played out within the terms of the particular cultural context. Thus, that depth narrative may resonate with the experience of others and give cultural meaning. If the story mythically succeeds, it transcends the particular culture even as it gives expression to it, even as the individual's experience is transcended in its expression. The archetypal story (myth) is not *im*personal; it is deeply personal and *trans*personal. "Mind" cannot be surgically separated from the body, nor can "myth" be extracted from life's meaning.

The question, then, is not *whether* myth is possible in contemporary life but *how* myth is manifested in today's experience. The archetypes are not specific, stamped-out figures inserted as signposts into significant psychological materials. Rather, the archetypes make up a precondition, appearing almost as a recognizable quality or dimension that may be filtered through any historical circumstance. Archetypal dimensions do not poke through like ill-fitting armatures in artistic works. Myth demands that color and texture of the entire body—bones and blood and fur. The "pure" state of the archetypal is in whatever state we discover it; the state in which I discovered it recently was in the improvisational play of some children. Where does one begin?

At home. Since I had slight trepidations about the project, I decided to cheat a little and ask my own children to supply a propitious beginning. My son, an eleven-year-old sometime dramatist, would have nothing to do with holiday pageantry. My daughter, seven, fascinated with visions of holy families, loved the idea. "Let's begin," she said calculatingly with her eye on a good role, "with Mary and the baby Jesus." "No," said her brother, "I wouldn't be in any play with Mary and Jesus." "Well," she retreated, "at least the three kings." "No!" Again she sought compromise. "At least Martin-Luther-King." Her brother hooted at her, but she defended her historical acumen by informing him that Martin-Luther-King was indeed one of the three kings who lived a Long Time Ago and said that everybody had to be nice and sit together and he came to visit the baby Jesus. Her brother told her she was dumb; I bogged down in bland thoughts about creative conflations and about how historical dramas frequently edge on excessive didacticism; and she went off to write her own play by herself. The unfinished manuscript rests at:

> Mary and Baby.
> Knock at door.
> *Who is it?*
> *Martin Luther King. I came to visit you.*
> *Oh good. Come in.*

I report this to emphasize that although myth is made in contemporary experience, it is not *inevitably* made. Just as I was desperately beginning to see "possibilities" in the script, her brother saw that there were none and finally agreed to cooperate. "Okay, you can't have Jesus, but you can have a god. I'll compromise." End of conversation. End of planning. End of the old mythological order. Nothing.

At the first cast meeting I bravely began with the quasi-lie that one of their company had suggested that in this play they were going to make up together there should be a god. Would anyone here like to be God? Six scoffs, two no-interests, but two enthusiastic volunteers. I immediately grasped at the straw gods and declared that both of them would be fine. I waited for objections, but monotheism is, apparently, an outmoded issue.

If we live in a culture without gods, without cohesive stories validating our culture and our place within it, then what sorts of stories will we make? The same old stories, the stories about being strangers to the story we already know. And the little drama created by these ten children suggests that today's stories may be about false gods who still authenticate human experience. Perhaps only fraudulent gods can genuinely express such times. The making of myth in contemporary conscious-ness seems to demand that it will carry its own parody within it, and certainly this drama company reinforced such a thought.

The six-year-old announced that he would be Buddha be-cause there was a statue of the Buddha on his mantel. The ten-year-old decided she would be the one with the thunderbolt. Without realizing it, the play was already made at this point; everything else simply unfolded from it. The new gods mounted a low table, looking awkward. I asked them to begin the play. They giggled and muttered like some dull, self-reflective divin-ities about what it was like to be a god and everyone became bored with their abstract theology. I suggested that since there was nothing else happening, they might choose to bring some-one else into the play (the others were restless).

> Zeus: *Let's create something.*
> Buddha: *What's that?*
> Zeus: *Let's make something out of these lumps of nothing* (pointing to the others, arousing laughter and interest).
> Buddha: (always more passive and receptive) *Okay, What?*
> Zeus: *Let's make* (prompting from future screeching angels) . . . *an angel.*

The play evolved in three quick, intense sessions. Additions and revisions were adapted and responded to by the entire group; but I noticed that the work was done by individuals modeling and creating with the group reinforcing. No one was able to follow a whim unless it resonated with the larger group, but the group was impotent unless activated by individual in-spiration.

> Buddha: (pause, mis-prompting from one of the older lumps of nothing attempting to be disruptive) . . . *An angle?*

The disruption, to the initial surprise of the older wits, was always incorporated into the drama. As Buddha developed his role over the three organizing sessions, he made angles with his fingers and elbows, reminding the director, at least, of ancient cosmographical pictures of the Creator inscribing the contours of the universe.

> Zeus: *No, an angel.*
> Buddha: *What's an angel?*
> Zeus: *I'll show you.*
> Future Angels: (screaming) *I am the angel.*
> Zeus: *Zap. Zap.*
> (Two angels.)

As it developed, the play opened with Zeus and Buddha on-stage. "Seven little lumps," as they called themselves and sometimes their drama, crawled in to music under drapery cloths of chaos, waiting for their acts of creation. The angels emerged from under their cloths and laughed. They were costumed in old nighties and foil-wrapped coat hanger wings, like the multitudes of less than heavenly hosts before them. They danced to a bit of "Nutcracker" and bumped into each other (renewing the question, how many *graceful* angels can dance on the head of a pin?). They fell over a bit of the stuff of creation and decided to make something. They gave each other orders and pulled and wadded the cloth. One clever lump named them "Miracle" and "Whip," and they fought over the names which were never used except in the programs. The names were accepted but not acclaimed. Some of the verbal play was too esoteric for the entire group and did not enter into common usage. All the great stories seem to have esoteric qualities that fall in and out of notice. I was interested to see that these esoteric dimensions are not always later interpretations but often part of the original textual fabric.

> Miracle: *I'll make the head.*
> Whip: *No, I will.*

This celestial quarrel, they happily realized, would result in the creation of the Two-Headed Cow. A ten-year-old had decided at the outset of the project that he was unwilling to be anything but a two-headed cow, deluding himself that he would be an insurmountable problem. He was then stuck with the role that he, and only he, had determined to be negative and unworkable. He was, by turns, happy and discontent with his part;

and it was finally his mother, as his wardrobe mistress, who had to take the most active adult part and suffered the only real difficulties of this play making. She had to help him costume himself. He wore a hooded sweatshirt which held an extra styrofoam head. The boy and the styrofoam wore matching horns and nose. And so the first earthly beast was born.

>   Two-Headed Cow: *Moo. Moo.*

The angels, doing the work of improvisational drama, which often does the work of dream, threw back the cloth and uttered their spontaneous pun:

>   Angels: (slapping their foreheads) *Holy Cow.*

Trying to hold center stage, they flitted on half-learned ballet steps to another lump.

>   Whip: *Let's make something else.*
>   Miracle: *Let's make a boy.*
>   Whip: *What's a boy?*

The pleasures of repetition were apparent. I should have realized that a creation formula was already in use.

>   Miracle: *Let's make legs.*
>   Whip: *I'll make the hands.*
>   Miracle: *I'll make a tongue. Stick out your tongue. I'll give him a tongue like ours.*

One angel modeled her tongue while the other modeled the tongue of the boy, the divine form and the particular creation. None of the children were struck by the profoundly different scenes between their creations of cow and boy. None of them had been corrupted by the Pauline letters. Cows could have two heads, but only human beings would speak with the tongues of angels. Even Buddha seemed to feel the moment and said with great solemnity, "They're making angel tongues." Improvisation offers the chance to perceive lively transformations of things turning into themselves and of the uncreated knitting itself into new inventions.

Boy stood up. No one in the play ever considered giving Boy anything more specific than his Everyman name. He was fourteen, tall in bib overalls, and the other, smaller characters looked upon him and uttered sounds of approval. He blinked his eyes and became a human being. He looked around with curiosity. He asked a rapid succession of questions about everything he saw. He asked the big questions that constitute the fundamental quest inherent in sacred texts from myth to improvisations:

Boy: *Who am I?*
Angels: *Boy.*
Boy: *Who are you?*
Angels: *Angels.*

There was obvious delight in their catechism.

Boy: (to angels) *Where did you come from?*
Buddha: (an admission) *We made them.*
Boy: *What are you?*
Zeus: *Gods.*
Boy: *What are gods?*
Buddha: *We make things.*
Boy: *Where'd you come from? Who made you?*

Pause. All the children were waiting for the answer; the air was still. But gods do not reveal the nature of Being so readily. In the silence and confusion, the Devil—as yet uncreated but already contriving—peeped from under his chaos blanket and prompted the gods: "You should say, 'God only knows.' " Buddha used the line and stole the show, though he had to be reminded with a nudge from Zeus' thunderbolt. They were uninhibited about giving suggestions and lines to one another. At each session of playmaking the characters enjoyed the reciprocal pleasures of making and watching, of "let there be" and "behold, it is good." They stepped in and out of the drama at will, but never out of the play. One of the problems with improvisational technique is that while it is so rewarding to the participants, some of the most significant features can be lost when translated into public performance. The audience did not learn that the words came to the God by means of the Devil's not-yet mouth.

Faced with the mystery, Boy did what humanity has always done.

Boy: *I'm going to make something myself.*

This, indeed, was the Creation of Man. Boy made himself by naming himself maker. The play is fabrication: the art of making and the art of lying, the art of making by lying. Homo faber then took up one of the lumps' cloths and began twisting and twirling it up into a spiral.

Zeus: *What are you doing?* (spoken with the authority of a sister, no mere god)
Boy: *I'm making something.* (trying to think of something) *I'm making a pot.*

The pot burst out from under her cloth and screamed, "I'm not going to be a pot, I'm a cat." In the final version she wore decorated brown paper under her cloth and at the proper moment "shattered" it and emerged. The Devil, still locked in chaos, supplied her name, "Platter Puss," worked out the dialogue, and explained the etymology. Myths, of course, are filled with language play and folk etymologies that point to the sacred nature and multiple dimensions of the words of the story. Again, the Devil was the source of the language play, but hidden from the audience.

Boy: *Because you came out of a pot and turned into a cat, I will call you Platter Puss.*

The order of creation was given. The gods created by their word (zap); the angels by dance and laughter—by imitation and invention; Boy created by shaping—by imitation and hubris. The creations of humanity seem to have a transformative power of their own, and by means of the word shift their shapes: pots become cats, experience becomes poetry. Creation, in this story, moved from the word to dance and back to the word. I was very content, my mind gathering golden boughs of comparisons, when—

Enter history. The Fall. "This play isn't any good. All we do is create things. That's boring." Well, I asked, what should happen next? They were quite right. There was no story without a break in the pattern. There is no mythic dimension without depth plunges into the meaning of humanity. Endless creation, gods begetting angels, angels begetting cows and boys, boys begetting pots, and pots begetting cats—it all begins to pall, like priestly chronologies from the ancient Near East. Creation myths are not in the creation, but in the fall or the change. There is no birth until there is death. (The alternative title they chose for their drama was "The Beginning and the End.") There is no story until there is humor or deceit.

The gods themselves were beginning to be bored, so they made devils to take the place of angels. "Zap, zap" and they created a Devil and a Demon. (The Devil was created mostly because he was begging to be a devil and promising to do something interesting to make the play better, and the Demon because she was little and they didn't know what else to do with her.) The Devil laughed fiendishly as he emerged and the Demon grinned—with two teeth missing.

Once on stage, though, the Devil had so many plans he couldn't think of one to put into action. It was his turn to be prompted. Zeus recalled that a story she had read about three wishes was good—the three wishes came from three hairs of the Devil's head. So this bit of plagiarism was unselfconsciously welcomed. The Demon was outfitted with a pendant made of nursery scissors. The Devil supplied the exposition for the audience and bent over to have three hairs cut from his red head. The Demon was demonically literal as she agonized to cut exactly three hairs. I explained to her that for the sake of theatre she could fake it and just flourish her scissors and pretend to cut hair. She could not. She cut exactly three hairs from the Devil's head.

Demon: *Here.*
Boy: *What's this?*
Demon: *Three wishes.*

Ah, she had made the metaphorical leap. She was after precision but not literalism after all. This plagiarism in the service of narrative form was the only such experience in the play. Poets have always chosen the familiar in the hope of the unknown. The actors plagiarized and produced a first-order experience from it. They stole the plot so that they could find out what was going to happen next.

"I've been here all this time and I'm not in the play yet," complained the one character left to emerge.

"I'll bring you in as soon as I have my wishes," said Boy, not wishing to relinquish his opportunity. He began to work on his wishes, thinking it through as ambitiously as if there were real devils giving him real opportunities. Quite spontaneously the characters began to advise him and to seek personal favors through Boy's wishes. This was one of the most difficult moments for the director. The scene had to be paced and staged so that the actors could maintain their look of frenzy but so that the audience could understand each character's advice or plea.

Zeus, with her Olympian mind, said that given three wishes Boy should ask for one wife, one daughter and one son. She (Zeus) was certain her advice would prevail and was self-satisfied with the tidy, pleasing conclusion she perceived she was bringing to the play. It was tempting for the director to lobby for Zeus' suggestion. It would be sure to tug at holiday sentimentality (and make up for the absence of the more holy family of Mary, Jesus, and Martin Luther King). However, the other characters were suspicious of domestic happily-ever-afters, and Boy vetoed his sister's plan.

Buddha didn't care for the direction the play was taking; he seemed to feel his power, his central role on the table top, was diminishing and asked boy NOT TO WISH FOR ANYTHING. I jumped in and told him about Buddha and extended the natural direction of his plea for non-striving and non-desire. All of the Buddhist phrases were ignored in performance, and Buddha kept his own high-pitched plea to wish for nothing in his own language and for his own reasons.

Platter Puss meowed and bounced around Boy begging for a mouse. When it occurred to her that there were three wishes, she begged for two mice, then three. Two-Headed Cow pleaded to have one of his heads removed.

The devils, those spirits of symbol-making, were the most vocal, inciting Boy to all the vices they could conjure.

At this point chaos threatened to submerge creation again (cosmic and dramatic). The director was searching for a way out, but they found it themselves. The two-headed cow and the cat were most irritating and strident, hanging on to Boy and screaming at him. He tossed them backward and said (to fellow actors more than to characters), "I wish you animals would shut up."

The Devil squealed and said, "That's your first wish—the animals have to shut up." Cat and cow obeyed as though they had been struck dumb by some Great Power. The director was nearly silenced, too, to see a play save itself—or at least to quiet itself down. Yet I could not resist pointing out the etiological message to the actors. "That must be why animals can't talk today." There was a flicker of interest from the children, but they were more interested in wishes. With the animals silenced the gods were able to hear their own commands again. Zeus and Buddha became so overbearing in their demands on the human soul that Boy exclaimed to them, "You gods get out of here." The Devil once more erupted in demonic laughter. "Your second wish, your second wish, the gods have to go."

Boy attempted to argue with this younger child. He had not intended his injunction as a wish. "Wait a minute, you're counting things as wishes when I don't mean them as wishes," never realizing that he was playing his part just as a thousand stories have played it out before him. Neither did he realize that no younger child is going to give up supernatural power so easily. So the Devil's decision prevailed with the cast and the gods went out, stage left. I unforgivably stopped the progress of the play again to tell them about *deus absconditus*.

The Devil, always clever and conscious that no one really cares about the death of god, playful and distracting, got us back in the mood with, "That's your second wish. Just ONE left." Boy realized that he had wasted two wishes, and we reached that inevitable point that always happens in these fairy tales—the lesser myths of luck and mismanagement of magic. Boy, feeling foolish and pressured by Devil and Demon on either side of him, put his hands to his head and moaned in a plea to the director, "I wish I had time to figure this out." The devils went wild, wild enough for me to channel it into some sort of dance for the scene.

Devil: *You wished for Time. That's your third wish.*
Time? How would we do that?
Is that me? Do I finally get to come into this play? asked the
   last man out.
Yes.
Okay. I'll be Time and wear a big cloak and a lot of clocks on
   me.
Boy: *Okay. Time, come in and end this play.* [!]

When the drama was performed before the audience, the
word "time" marked a sudden, palpable change in mood. The
characters stood silently as Time entered to music, flourishing
his cloak.

Time: (as lugubriously as he was able) *Did you call? It's TIME.*

He explained to the others that time can make one die. He
touched the animals and they fell over dead. In the final version they crawled back under their cloths to become "lumps"
again. He explained to Boy that time would make him old. In
the actual presentation Time wrapped his cloak quickly around
Boy's head and fitted him surreptitiously with a white wig and
beard. Boy backed up, felt his face and groaned, "What's the
matter with me?"

Time: *You made time, you wished for time, so you have to die.*
Boy: *I'm old. I'm going to die.*

The moment was as poignant as when Gilgamesh sat down
to weep. Then, the director, like a priestly gloss, asked what
good things Time was bringing. Time stood there, ticking off
nothing. So with the animals silenced and dead, the gods banished, the devils once more began to furnish answers, now for
Father Time. They said time was needed to bake a cake, for
music, for doing plays . . . .

Apparently, too, for boredom. Time interrupted them and
said, "And time for plays to end." Later, before the audience,
the cliché was interpolated, "And time for all good things to
come to an end." Imaginal time and space, once manifested
into ordinary dimensions, does not, of course, permit conclu-

sions but continues to enhance the creation of consciousness. After the performance Zeus wore her painted stars on her face all day long, masking her ordinary self. She had rediscovered the ways we mingle fictions in order to arrive at truths.

Theatre's first act is to reproduce the FIRST ACT. The play is always a divine disguise reflecting creation by creating reflections. The masquerade divines realities. But in all my experience with adults in improvisational drama the world was never created. The performances have been occasionally metaphysical, frequently archetypal and mythic, but never a Hymn to Creation. These children, both by accident and by design, began at the beginning and brought it to one of many endings. Their experience of mythmaking would not be ours. Part of contemporary existence is knowing that although we can't make up a new story, each time we tell the story it will be different. We cannot stop making myths any more than we can stop inventing ourselves.

Their myth was not merely the emergence of ego—creation and the fall in the simple sense—nor the validation of community—corporate ego. Their myth was more; it was what myth always is and it did what myth always does: it merged depth and daylight and bestowed a new order on the chaos of both. Myth is a symbolic narrative that gives order to chaos, truth to tales, and the fancy of this un-Christmas play did just that.

There is no doubt that the play functioned to create and unite a community of players, although it did much more. They felt positive about themselves, respected one another, asked for more—to be continued.

As for ritual, the companion of many myths, the kids continue to request *another* play. Our ritualistic repetitions are acted out in uniqueness, invention, and spontaneous laughter. To achieve the mythical in the postmodern age is not to imitate or attempt to capitulate to preconscious forms. It is to bring the fullness of conscious experience from depth awareness.

The modern age determined its difference from the past by somehow attempting to sever contact with depth. The age we are entering now is not so existential, nor so fragmented. We are coming into a time in which we can be at once archetypally attuned, existentially conscious, aesthetically sensitive, and religiously awakened.

The *myths* of the postmodern age may resemble children's play: archetypal and comic, ritualistic and spontaneous. Comic self-consciousness is one of the significant ways that our contemporary myth-making is manifested. It is the soul that laughs, and laughter is created when depth makes mockery of time and when time makes fun of unconsciousness.

God and Moses are no longer responsible for the Hebrew canon, yet the antiquated notion persists that myth must be more than the work of human, articulate, creative individuals assisted by their communal experience. When Yahweh wrote the Ten Commandments with his own finger, myths seemed to be the spontaneous outflow of societies that were witness to such an event. As our perspectives on the stories change, our perspectives on how stories are made change. Stories and the making of them are a double-helix structure. To untangle them is to damage their life force. The making of the story is the telling of the story, the retelling is making it new. Myths in our time are likely to be ephemeral, improvised.

The cast of wonderfully individualistic gods and creatures meshed and merged. Everyone knew the structure and perceived the need for it. At play we are most conscious, clever, sharp, yet most deeply unconscious and playing out. The playing of this group was at once new and ancient. If we are to find myth in contemporary times, it is not a story without contemporary consciousness, but rather a story which creates from timeless patterns *and* contemporary wit. Dreams are made up of the strange and the familiar. History, like myth, is made of metaphor. They are both made of essentially aesthetic patterns. Stories are made by time encountering the gods, or the gods inventing and confronting time.

And the next time we find ourselves mismanaging some sudden, ten-minute epic, we can anticipate the discovery of what we can't quite remember now—what comes next.

The Flea's Shoes
Mistrust of Image

A 136-year-old man dozed through a movie of his own life. He did, however, enjoy his party, and did reminisce for those who wanted to listen to him. Perhaps he was still busy making his life, making up his life.

The concept of the world without imagination is euphemistically referred to as "reality"; but as the poet Wallace Stevens said, "the absence of imagination has itself to be imagined."[1] If imagination forms reality, how can we characterize reality as something devoid of that which gives rise to it? The method for dissolving the paradox is to affirm it, to enter into it; that method is sometimes called art and sometimes religion. The images we create in turn create us. The ways that we image the world (out of our imaginations) in turn give us the perspectives (images) we have on ourselves (the imaginal).

Religion and art are not precisely equivalent terms but relational perspectives. In a secularized culture particularly, art comes to be not an aesthetic expression of religious consciousness but a conflation of the two. In dualistic worldviews, the arts can belong to the "other" and be suspect, dangerous; or, subsequent to secularization, religion itself seems to originate in the "other" and seems amorphous, intangible, fugitive; the arts may then appear more tangible, more reliable. Although dualistic religion seems inevitably to inauthenticate itself, it wavers about which side of its partitioned mind the arts belong to.

Art, like religion, may be framed (or institutionalized), placed on a pedestal (or set apart and made taboo); but the distinctions or boundaries between them have been smudged and mingled throughout time. Not only the Romantics, who conflated truth and beauty, nor the ancient Egyptians, who made their arts the transitional doorway into eternity, nor the Bantu, who play the game of finding the hidden metaphor between apparently unrelated things, but all of us, forever, have made art to make ourselves; that is, it has been the expression of, the form of, and the nature of, religion.

Our iconoclastic heritage, though, has given us an odd attitude toward our art, and an implicit, but seldom recognized, companion attitude toward the sacred. Perhaps one of the ways to explore our religion is to look at our arts. Definitions of art may be the outer forms of descriptions of religion.

Certainly the great creation myths are celebrations of the arts. In one of these, we were born from a potter's wheel; an Egyptian god whirled us out of clay. We are fundamentally a work of art. Another god, a feminine deity, forged us out of metal, and if we listen carefully, some warm nights, what we thought were crickets is the goddess hammering out new human beings. She is an artist; we have been forged. One of the most playful creation myths comes from the Brihad-aranyaka Upanishad and tells of the oneness who in order to have delight (to play) separated into two. They copulated; but to trick him she turned herself into a cow. He metamorphosed into a bull, and they copulated. Cows came into the universe. She ran off again, turning herself into a fast mare, he transforming himself into a great stallion, and horses were born. They repeated their play until all of creation, right down to the ants, was created. Another creation myth informs us that Our Great Father, who is a mere appearance, a nothing, had a dream, another nothing. And He who is appearance only grasped onto the dream, the phantasm, and held onto the thread of the dream by thought. He thought about what was at the bottom of the dream and found it was nothing. I have attached to and connected with nothing, he said, and stamped upon the nothing like a fluff of cotton until it was a solid earth. Then he spat upon it until the forests grew and the seas were full. Then he lay down upon it and reached up and made the blue sky and the clouds. Our most fundamental stories, the creation stories, are stories of play—or what we call art. The creation of the world, all the world over, is made from the play of gods, potting, forging, dreaming, imagining, and making love. Play (or art) is turning one thing into another: mud into man, gods into horses and horses into love, dreams into earth. Dualistic culture demeans and degrades the creation and creativity.

Limiting our conversation to merely the visual arts, and those visual arts that have been claimed to be primarily aesthetic rather than functioning as other things, we can move along the continuum toward the sacred. How can we discuss the visual arts without a referent—a picture? Let's begin with a painting: a traditional, framed, two-dimensional work. Here is the frame. Please provide the art: imagine the painting.

(Do you feel confident that you did not overemphasize the dark tones? Should you extend the rhythm here with a touch of vivid color? No? Well, have it your way.) In other words, our framed imaginary painting is set here as a reminder for us to dispose of questions of formal requirements, that is, whatever concrete elements make up art, and to further remind us that art takes place in the mind. Admire once more the painting you have made, and we will agree that this painting is in your mind even if we may not be willing to say that it represents your frame of mind.

I would offer as a preliminary definition of art, then, that the object is the locus of inspiration, the focal point of concretizing the inspiration, and the place of re-evoking that inspiration in the minds of viewers; but that art, whether made or only imagined, is in the mind.

DEFINITION I: Art is only in the head.

What we think is beautiful, significant, or interesting is informed by our social, political, religious assumptions, by our worldview. This in turn provides our first description of *religion*, that the sacred is in the mind. Our social, political, religious assumptions are translated into what we think is beautiful, significant, or interesting.

Play, art, or religion, are not lower things that take place "only in the head," inferior to the rational realm. They are, instead, the acts and thoughts that incorporate the rational without being bound by the rules set down by the rational.

On the first level of play—and we all begin life as players, as artists—the things that we make are real. A child knows that Santa Claus, the Easter Bunny, the Tooth Fairy, are real. It took my daughter several years to learn how to respond to the query, "What are you going to be when you grow up?" She consistently answered, "An angel or an Easter Bunny." Although her selections were admired, it was clear she was not ready to imagine the meaning of "grown up." Causality ranked low in her cosmic scheme; everything that came, came in the night. Early one morning, the day of her father's oral defense, she came slipping into our room and asked, "Did it come?" "What?" asked her father. "Your Ph.D. Is it here?" The Ph.D Fairy, after all, must be the Tooth Fairy's younger sister.

Children, however, mature and go from simple belief to (simple) nonbelief. Our girl entered the age of rational skepticism. She announced frequently and emphatically that there is NO Santa Claus, no Easter Bunny, no Tooth Fairy. She had arguments and proofs; she was as vehement as the iconoclastic Reformationists in their accusations against the Church. But one night, she asked us accusingly, "Where are they?" "What?" "Where do the parents keep the teeth?" "What teeth?" "I know there is no Tooth Fairy; I know the parents get them. But I can't find them. I've looked everywhere. Where do the parents keep the teeth?" She had reached the age of reason; but she had also reached the limits of her reason. The need for play was so great, surely the teeth couldn't be discarded. They must be kept in a special or sacred place. After all, the taking of teeth, replacing them with coins, is a divine trick, a play, a transformation, even if parents do it. At this point, when we discover there is no great repository of teeth in any sacred ark, that the world of the literal is as confining as literalizing the imaginary, it is then that symbolic consciousness emerges. After iconoclasm, breaking down those false stories, we can go back and learn the ways in which the false stories are true. We can learn to tell stories again, incorporating both myth and reason, in order to reveal a peculiar structure of the world. To create the universe—as the gods did and as we do—is to interpret, select, emphasize, order, all that which makes up reason and imagination. The same child who uncovered the Tooth Fairy fraud and searched for the lost cache of baby teeth, subsequently discovered puppy teeth on the carpet, and along with an old buffalo tooth, she carefully wrapped them and took them to school. Understanding where they came from, the processes that brought them there, and yet finding they retained their power as *teeth*, a symbolic power, she grew from being acted upon to being actor, no longer played upon, but playing, no longer the point at which stories are directed, but the place where they are generated. Returning from school, she reported the spectrum of reactions from the children, recounted the information she had dispensed, and recalled the stories she had spun. She had rescued the ancient buffalo and her own puppy from the symbolic (or sacred) ignominy she herself had suffered from parents who did not keep the relics secured in the ark of her imaginal world. She put the teeth in a box. Symbolic understanding is the understanding that, as Norman O. Brown has said, "Symbolism conveys both absence and presence. To see three truths with the same mind: things are real, unreal, and neither real nor unreal."[2] The child moved from literalizing the fantasy, to iconoclastically denying it, to finally merging them in a symbolic apprehension.

DEFINITION II: We have sent Bach into outer space. Will the aliens ask, "Yes, but is it art?"

Our aesthetic judgments begin with a world view that informs us as to what is beautiful, just as our *religious* perspectives inform us of what is true. We send Bach into outer space to communicate to possible intelligences about the nature of our culture, while at the same time in popular theories and messages the claims proliferate that our cultures, particularly our religions, originated in outer space. One of the most remarkable and baroque forms of iconoclasm, of culture shattering, is the popular notion of aliens transmitting to us or infusing us with our grand expressions of heart and mind. It iconoclastically works against the gentle pride that sends forth Bach into the sonar universe. At the same time, perhaps the "outer space" hoax, sincere as it is, is merely the inevitable parody resulting from a mythological tradition that claims that an utterly transcendent yet simplistically anthropomorphic god not only created the physical universe, but also injected into that creation all the thoughts and designs possible.

Leonardo da Vinci was attracted to the theory of the Golden Section, which sought the mystery of harmony through this principle:

```
         a            b
    / ---------- / -------------------- /
```

The smaller segment is to the larger segment as the larger is to the whole. And today there are quantifiers who find such systems reassuring and measure up the great and not-so-great works of art. Proportion surely must have something to do with beauty, but:

DEFINITION III: Can a is to b as b is to ab really be the key to the secret of Mona Lisa's smile?
Or,
Mona Lisa is smiling because she has just found out the definition of art.

Check your painting again, the one you projected into the frame on the first page. Does it conform to the standard of the Golden Section? It well may. But many things are made which would conform to that harmony but fall short of what we might want to call art. Conversely, the Golden Section is a frequent, but not universal, formal principle in objects that we would consider art. We know that form is the basic constituent of art but that form cannot be taken out of its larger context and retain its total aesthetic value. Again, then, art takes place in the imagination—in visualizing more than what is visual. *Religion* is that paradox which inherently gives form as value to all our acts and thoughts, but cannot be extracted or separated out from anything else.

DEFINITION IV: All art is conceptual art.

We remember Picasso saying that he painted as he thought, not as he saw. It is something that all of us do; Picasso was able to name it and know it. Or, as Picasso is reported to have responded when someone remarked that his portrait of Gertrude Stein didn't look like her, "That's all right. It will." And it did. Or James Joyce's friend, listening in Paris to "Work in Progress," which would become *Finnegans Wake,* admitted to him finally, "Jimmy, what you're doing is not literature. It's beyond literature." He responded as did Picasso, "That's all right, it will be." And that is what it has become, informing all of modern literature.

DEFINITION V: Art transcends its environment.

DEFINITION VI: Art creates the reality that it lives in.
Oscar Wilde really said it much better, when he claimed, "Life imitates art."

My daughter came home one day with a grade school joke. Unintentionally, and unforgivably, I ruined the joke. It went like this:

> Daughter: *This is my pet flea. Would you like to see him dance and do gymnastics?*
> Me: *Yes.*
> Daughter: *Then hold his shoes.* (She laboriously pantomimes untying six miniature shoes and places them in my palm.) *Be very careful while you hold them; don't let them spill out.*
> Me: *Okay.* (And she folds my hands up as though it contains three matched pairs of tiny tennis shoes.)
> Daughter: *Watch now. Okay, Flea, dance. See him flip. Now he's over here, now he's on one leg. Do you like his tricks?*
> Me: *Yes.*
> Daughter: *Do you really believe there's a flea?*
> Me: *Yes.*

I regretted my answer as soon as I saw my error and her disappointment. The rational person—the grade-school jokester—would say, "Of course not. There's no flea there." I should have said that I didn't believe in the flea (the customary role of the straight man) so that she could deliver the withering punch line to the fool, "Then why are you holding his shoes?" Instead, she screamed at me, "You wrecked it. Then give me back his shoes!" She tried to take back the nonexistent shoes I was keeping safe in my fist, that belonged to the flea that wasn't there.

I was struck, after my guilt passed for failing to have wit enough to be straight man-fool for the joke, that she, too, was unable to play the game without imagining the flea and his shoes so strongly that although she knew there was no *actual* flea (the point of the joke), there was indeed an *actual image* of the flea—with acrobatic skills and tennis shoes. The image is real, even if founded on nothing more substantial than a non-flea. She didn't get the joke either. It's a joke for the unimaginative. The real joke is on the literalist.

DEFINITION VII: Art is imagination. It is an attempt to express the inexpressible, the unique, the significant, the more than visible.

Of course, in talking about the visual arts, we cannot deny that there is *something* there. *Religions* claim the ineffable, but their claims are fabricated from available materials, from what is *there*. *Religion* is described by its claim, not by the ineffable, the object of its claim.

DEFINITION VIIa: Art is imagination embodied.
Or,
Art is the locus of the coming together of thing and mind.

Whatever it is we call art disavows dichotomies of imagination and technology. We require of our artists the height of technical expertise and the profoundest of imaginative awareness. Yet it is almost as if a work of art were not the embodiment of its creator's point of view, but, once created, had a point of view of its own. People with resistances to unfamiliar works of art suspect that they may be "taken in." Indeed, art pulls, takes, sucks us into another perception, a way of seeing and knowing we had not encountered before.

And yet, before I am accused of being Romantic or post-Romantic, I must say that there is nothing extraordinary about art, the artist, or the connoisseur.

DEFINITION VIII: Art is so ordinary, so mundane, it is an essential ingredient in life.
Or,
DEFINITION VIIIa: Art is that essential ingredient of life that makes the ordinary special, or even unique.

Likewise, *religion* has been described as an overwhelming awakening into the saturated or unique quality of experience. Without art there would be a falling away, a decline from what it means to be human. Perhaps without *religion,* in its most basic form, there would be no awakening into what it can mean to be human.

DEFINITION IX: I don't know if it's art, but I know what I lack.

When we say "art," we find ourselves with a troublesome term. Even when we limit the term to refer exclusively to the realm of the visual arts, we are confronted immediately with the question whether we are referring to the artist (the maker), the product (the object), or the viewer (is it, indeed, in the eye of the beholder?)—or to some mingling of making, made, and re-making. Since the art that is the reference piece here is your own imaginary painting on the first page, it seems that we will have to commingle them.

DEFINITION X: There is no art unless it is seen (visual art); with each seeing it is re-created, and for the first time.

Sometimes we feel distressed at the false snobbery of the artist over the patron. The patron, we must remember, is not merely the person with the purse, but is also an artist, participating in the creative act by seeing. The viewer is not a passive recipient, but is engaged in imaginative dialogue with the maker. The art collector or art appreciator (as opposed to the mere investor), is also an artist making art.

But if I can't trust you to see what I have made the way I meant it, or if you can't trust me to see what you made the way you intended—what is art anyway?

DEFINITION XI: Art is like a flea's shoes.

And *religion* is the footprints made by gods, the impress of image and message. We find ourselves, like so many of our ancestors, mistrusting the image. Our consciousness is iconoclastic. Although iconoclasm generates a reforming, vitalizing force in religious awareness, in the western world it has meant, as well, a betrayal of the aesthetic.

The mistrust of the visual image winds, like a double helix, through the structural heritage of the western mind. From both the Hebrew and Greek (Platonic) traditions, there is a suspicion regarding the image; religiously or philosophically our tradition bears the message: beware of pictures.

The Hebrew tradition is famous for its prohibition of the image. The religion of Yahwism was surrounded by cultures that were highly imagistic, cultures in which the visual arts were a key element in worship and cultural institutions. Perhaps partially in response to the struggle against these seductive religions, the Hebrew tribes made it one of their fundamental commandments that there would be no molten or graven images. Yahweh could be worshipped without icon, without image. Everyone recalls the story of Moses descending the mountain with the tablets of the law and discovering that in his absence the people had melted their jewelry and made a "golden calf." Moses, angered, broke the tablets of the commandments, smashed the golden bull into a fine powder, strewed it on the water, and made the people drink it. This breaking of the image, or "iconoclasm," is one of the most forceful and recurrent paradigms in the Judaeo-Christian tradition.

Religiously, images have been used to remind worshippers of the divine referent in the image, to offer a place of sympathetic alignment between the human and the divine or between the secular and the sacred, or, finally, to offer a place where the divine referent might actually dwell in this likeness or symbolic reminder. These human works were seldom considered gods or idols in a simplistic sense. They were not intended as literal likenesses of gods, but were objects where gods might agree to or be persuaded to come. Everything from bone carvings to stone churches might be such sacred art. The western family of religions, Judaism, Christianity, and Islam, has maintained an ambivalence toward sacred art that has, of course, influenced the history of secular arts within each culture.

The Christian church developed a remarkable iconographic tradition, and God himself was imagined as an artist—musician, weaver, potter, painter, poet, architect.

DEFINITION XII: Art may be made by one who retreats from imagining the artist as a god but who may well imagine god as artist.

The Christian tradition, like its parent, Judaism, struggled with the image. Many early Christians theologized that there was a radical dualism between flesh and spirit, between the earth and the divine. Everything earthly and everything made on earth was a snare to trap the susceptible. This influence, connected to concern about corruption in the church, led to a number of reforming movements, culminating with the Protestants in the sixteenth century, who were sometimes as passionate as Moses in their iconoclasm. The breaking of the images which it was feared would lead people into idolatry also demonstrated sometimes a troublesome ambivalence. Art historians tell us of a picture of the crucifixion in which the image of Christ had been torn to shreds, while, ironically, the figure of the thief had been left intact. Seeing and believing have not had the easy fellowship the folk proverb would have us think. What was seen and visible in the world of the early church was not what was depicted. What was depicted was the superior reality of the invisible. That is, until the iconoclasm of the Reformation, when along with the interest in the natural world of light and perspective developed in the Renaissance, the unseen world receded and the secular world and secular artist emerged. Among the accomplishments of the Reformation, however, is the particularly troublesome reassertion of dualism.

One telling example of the emergence of secular art is a panel of Christ and the twelve apostles, that in 1524 had to be removed from a chapel in Zurich. The panel was not destroyed, however. We learn that the city of Zurich had been painted as the background; thus, Christ and the apostles were merely painted out, and the city and landscape that the sacred figures had concealed were filled in. Art transferred its attention from the heavens to the earth; and, pentimento, the gods disappeared behind the secular landscape.[3]

The visible world has been interpreted in a variety of ways; style is part of the temperament and the knowledge of an age. On the Greek side of our tradition, there was a mistrust of the visual image and of the artist. The artist, according to Plato, was inspired, but the inspiration was not trustworthy.

More importantly, Plato's view of art was that it was an imitation of the world, which itself was an imitation of the ideal forms. This hierarchy of reality meant that the artist could paint only an inferior representation, which was itself an inferior representation of the Ideal Pattern, or Reality. What, then, is the inspiration that the artist receives?

Enter the muse. These divine inspirers taught their poets, their artists, not to imitate ordinary reality but to skip right over it to create the essence of higher truth. This higher truth, or intimation of the Ideal, may wear the clothing of ordinary reality but somehow manifests the secret of the reality superior to the mundane.

One never knew whether the muse was inspiring toward truth or merely glittering fancy.

DEFINITION XIII: Art is the means of telling lies in order to reveal the truth.

We need not be troubled in our contemporary world with the "pleasing shapes that devils may take," or with the lies of the muse. We might do well, though, to try to catch a glimpse of our own muse.

In the frame below, make nothing. Instead, draw a picture of your muse *outside* the frame. Muses, from what I've been told by artists, children, liars, and wisepeople, are seldom

dreamy ladies in gauzy nighties; muses may come as the rust rings left by unwashed frying pans, as Thomas Jefferson, or as a ridiculous joke that failed.

If we remember the muse not as the personification of the creative principle but as the artist herself, we may be able to catch glimpses of her, have conversations with her, or she may even whisper the secret of art into our ears.

DEFINITION XIV: Art is that which is made by the muse.
Or,
Art is that which is mused upon by the muse.
Or,
Art is that which amuses the muse.

They are definitions that may make the muse cringe; after all, if we substitute *religion* for *art* and *the divine* for *the muse*, the description of religion has nearly disintegrated. Art is whatever has strength and integrity enough to make the muse stop and think, and to make her laugh. Perhaps our *religions* aspire to such notions.

At least we almost know what art isn't. When someone says, "Boy, I sure wouldn't hang that in my living room," we know we may be close. Art is probably too disturbing, too surprising, too demanding to hang around quietly in the living room.

Although art is made within the conventions of its own period, it is also made as a challenge to those conventions. It goes beyond what it expresses best. After we changed our cultural minds about art, painted out divinities, and disallowed goddesses from having a hand in our work, we came to a convention called "realism," which has sometimes confused us on the question of what art is about; just as dualism, robbed of the divine or secularized, can encourage a worldview about as satisfying as a glossy advertisement.

"Realism" itself is based upon stylistic convention as much as are the wood carvings of tribal Africa, the wall reliefs of the ancient Mesopotamians, or the painted miniatures of the early Christians. What's "real" is determined by what is important, what is noticed.

Recognizing conventional reality as style rather than "things as they actually are" is sometimes elusive. Everyone recalls the story of the Taoist philosopher Chuang Tzu who dreamed that he was a butterfly and ever after wondered whether he was a man who had dreamed he was a butterfly or a butterfly who was now dreaming he was a man.

Another Taoist tale, less familiar, troubles us more about art and reality. There was a king who was watching an artist. He asked the artist, "What do you like to paint best?" The artist replied, "Ghosts." "What," asked the king, "is most unpleasant to paint?" The artist answered quickly, "Dogs." "Why?" The artist explained to the king, "Well, when I paint ghosts I can do anything I want. No one I know has ever seen a ghost. But when I paint a dog, I have to be very careful to get everything in the right place and make my picture look like a dog. Everyone I know has seen a dog. That's why I like to make ghosts and do not like to make dogs." (Look back at the picture you made of the muse. Is she just a ghost?) Reality, however, is not as simple as the appearance of a dog. There is more to depict, and ghosts inhabit the paintbrushes. The imaginal is the recognition that we create our realities. To look at a dog, let alone to paint it, is to create the dog. The Taoist painter lived in a fluid reality, where nouns and verbs traded places. When we draw a picture of the muse, we too are beginning to live in the connections, where things transform.

Style is the defense of a worldview. Comparing a magazine of fifty years ago with a current, comparable example, readily informs us how much our expectations and ideas of what is pleasing or acceptable have altered. Perhaps these trivial examples of our rapidly shifting ephemeral culture can serve to show us how we have shifted, in deeper ways, our senses of self.

DEFINITION XV: Art is interpretation.

DEFINITION XVa: Art is selection, which is interpretation.
Selection itself is the process of interpretation.

DEFINITION XVb: To mark is to remark.
Everything is commentary. We perceive and we select. That is, we invent.

E. H. Gombrich has noted that perception is a constructive act rather than a receptive or analytic one. Visual perception and visual imagination, he says, belong to the same human process. To see is to make. *Religion* can be described as interpretation—a constructive act.

DEFINITION XVI: We may not make what we see, but what we see makes us.

I once recognized one of the manifestations of my muse because she changed me. One night, with an attack of insomnia, I got up to do some bibliographic work as a soporific. As I sat down at my desk, I noted my shadow playing across the edges of one of my favorite pictures on the wall, changing it. That shadow seemed to form an independent picture of another being. I turned then to a journal and stumbled across an article about the legend of the invention of painting.

There she was. The muse. She came as a sentimentalized, romantic legend concerning a woman named Dibutade or Butades, who was moved by the parting of her lover. She sorrowed at his leaving and, as he departed, traced the outline of his shadow on the wall. There in the lamplight (or moonlight— the versions differ) she chose—not to detain her lover, nor to mourn him, nor even merely to hold him in her memory. She chose rather to serve her memory with invention; she chose to *imagine* the memory of that moment of separation in a new way. She traced the outline of a shadow and made a new thing. This narrative stood as the emblem for the invention of painting, but worked within me as the embodiment of something more.

The muse seldom comes when called. Especially since we know that muses do not really exist—this makes their jobs much harder. She will insist, however, on informing us of her definition of art:

DEFINITION XVII: Art is the work that is play.

She may even appear as a flea wearing tennis shoes. She can't, however, be framed. Color her outside the lines. Take another look at her as you made "her" near the frame above.

6

The Man-and-Woman-Eating Plant
Imagery and Iconoclasm

A small girl drew a picture of a person engulfed by baroque vines blossoming from a hanging pot. "This," she said, "is a Man-and-Woman-Eating Plant." And explained to me, "Most of the time you don't have to worry, because most of them are just man-eating plants." With that image the child analyzed the language (demythologized, discriminated, or acted iconoclastically) and wrote herself back into the cosmic drama (remythologized, synthesized, or reimagined).

In a secularized yet dualistic culture, women are still charged with being unclear and unclean, irrational and nonlinear, mad and bloody. In many stories they are left out, invisible, insignificant, perhaps even *inedible* in a world of "man-eating plants."

The ancient stories repeat the notion that the feminine is the transgressor. The curious quality of many of those stories is that it is through transgression that creative work takes place or divine will is accomplished. Cultures sometimes make themselves whole by the holes pierced through the social and cosmological fabric, by the pollutions, the deviations, the excesses of the feminine, the awkwardnesses of the fool, or the play of angels. It is by exceeding the bounds, according to our mythologies, that we fabricate new boundaries. It seems that we are living in a time that is iconoclastic as well as integrative, disintegrative as well as iconogenerative. It may be that there are no new stories, the old ones keep erasing themselves and rewriting themselves; and perhaps this is one of those times of erasure and rewriting.

ᕦ

I am not suggesting and would not suggest that the ancient stories provide models by which we can pattern ourselves, any more than I would claim that it would be possible to write new, original stories. I am suggesting that the ancient stories resonate poetically with our pretenses toward a new story.

The human impulse to preserve the world as we know it, to make rigid its walls, secure its borders, is a religious activity. Religions reassure, reacquaint, realign us with the known and keep us safe from the chaos of new perception. But other religious activities break down walls, rearrange the borders, celebrate chaos by writing its programs and discovering its resemblances (and hence order) to ourselves. The religion of preservation tells us who we are; the religions of disorientation force us to create ourselves.

There are, at the heart of every culture, base metaphors—or metaphorical potentialities—that form everything else within that culture. This imaginal latent power engenders and arranges all aspects of culture, ranging from ethics to garments, from relationships to trinkets. This metaphorical potentiality is playful—is play itself.

Ancient Hebrew laws reflect a prior imaginal base of reality. Ethical restraints regarding the stranger, directives of hospitality, are found in the metaphorical memories of a wandering people; laws about women are based upon the patriarchal worldview; laws concerning other peoples are based upon a model of conflict and conquest.

Monotheism itself, a significant and profound religious development, may be rooted in the image of a god who, unlike his neighbors, had no wife, sister, consort, no theogony, no palace. Yahweh originated anthropomorphically enough, but his mythic realm was sparsely populated and furnished. This god lacked stories about himself except for those which told of his meddling with his creatures. Certainly this mythic consciousness nourished the concepts of sacred history, even of the religious imperatives of love. In the Hebraic attempt to distinguish themselves from their neighbors, monotheism emerged ("Thou shalt have no other gods before me"); in attempts to distinguish themselves from their conquerors, universal monotheism emerged ("How shall we worship the Lord in a strange land?"). Image precedes message; the mythic makes the ethic.

These great models have within themselves a fluidity, an ambiguity, a capacity to dissolve, disassemble, or dissemble. Indeed, they are not models as such, but preconditions for models, which can rearrange themselves as they construct the cultures they form, or be undone by the cultures made from them. The culture of patriarchy, after all, is by means of its constituent qualities unraveling itself and weaving another view of reality.

The story of Rachel sitting on her father's household gods iconoclastically subverts the laws crystallized by her descendants about honoring parents, lying, and consummately, the "ethical" prohibition derived from ancient taboos surrounding menstrual blood. Jacob decided to flee Laban's household after having tricked his father-in-law one too many times. When Laban realized that his household gods were missing—his hold on his property threatened—he pursued Jacob and Rachel. Searching all of the goods while Jacob played or remained the innocent, Laban finally came to Rachel, sitting in her tent. Asking her to get up, she replied that she could not: "The way of women is upon me." Her father retreated and the joke, Rachel's playful use of the taboo, furthered sacred history.

The treachery of females is a prominent cultural metaphor, and by the treachery of females Yahweh's sacred history is unrolled: by Eve's transgression history and freedom begin; by Rebecca's deception upon blind Isaac the divine will for the patriarchal lineage is assured; by Jael's treachery with the enemy general Sisera the Hebrew warriors "win"; by Tamar's disguise her father-in-law Judah was tricked into overcoming one law and complying with a greater one—to provide a dead kinsman his children. These stories propel the sacred paradigms of the people; and great stories also suggest their own revisions or distortions. Curiosity, choice, action on the part of these symbolic feminine figures disrupt the known. Stories carry more meaning than their narrators openly know. The stories we have inherited, which have bound us to a vision of reality, may also participate in the iconoclasm essential to remythologizing ourselves. As we tell other stories the old ones are revised; we see in them narrative threads and colors before unrecognized. It is not only learned rabbis who keep the stories going by creatively interpreting—that is, by making them new stories; but anyone who hears a story and remembers it is not only carrying, not only commenting upon, but also making the tradition anew.

Paradigms of reality shift their borders. The paradigm of combat may never give way; dualism may be as ingrained in human consciousness as having two hands or distinguishing between morning and evening. But stories of the feminine, particularly, frequently undermine that dualism; out of the two, they offer a third. One of the most beloved stories of the Virgin tells of a clerk in the Church of Saint Peter who was devoted to the Virgin.

> One night he noticed that there was not enough oil to keep her light lit through the night. Since it was Saint Peter's church, there was an abundance of oil which had been left before the image of Peter. So the clerk took a little oil from Saint Peter and gave it to the Virgin, to keep her lamp lit until morning.
> That night a terrible dream came to the clerk; Saint Peter appeared and said, "She has plenty of attendants in many places. This is the only place where I receive such devotions. You have done this thing to me, but just remember, I am the keeper of the Gate of Heaven. When you are ready to enter, I will bar the way." The poor man was greatly distressed, but he did not relent in his passionate devotions to the Virgin, even though he knew he would be locked out of Heaven by the offended Gatekeeper.

When he lay on his deathbed, however, the Virgin appeared to him and said, "You have never departed from your faithfulness to me. I know that Saint Peter's Gate is locked, but when you arrive before Heaven just come around to the side. I will let you in my window. For although Peter's gate is narrow and straight, come in through my window, for my window is wide."

Through the Virgin's window enter the comic and the erotic. The model is revised. The Virgin herself is an iconic celebration of the feminine, rising in the midst of hierarchical, dualistic, and apocalyptic religion. In the contemporary world as women enter and revise mainstream institutions, the feminine paradigm informs and reforms the world. The windows will be opened. (This does not refer to women who want to enter and succeed in the mainstream hierarchy, nor does it exclude men from the feminine paradigm. It is a question of perception, of the imaginal, and not of genitals.)

In contrast to the social subordination of women in cultural history, stories within that heritage, ranging from the oldest strata of tradition to the most elaborated forms of literature, depict women or feminine beings who are active and vital. They are the creators and interpreters of the experiences that form the deepest structures of their culture. The implication is not, it seems to me, about a lurking vestigial matriarchy, but about the imaginal, creative sources of culture itself. The implication is not so much about women and men, for stories do not offer "role models" but create every model within the culture. The "feminine" in the paradigmatic stories is that which generates religion or the sacred.

There is nothing, after all, that is outside of or separable from "ordinary life." Those elements of life that are marked or re-marked, imagined or remembered, are made extraordinary. But the extraordinary is the ordinary celebrated.

Mothers used to warn their daughters, "Stay out of the cucumber patch during your time." Without explanation, it was implicit that menstrual blood was a powerful pollutant to those poor phallic fruits. Though we are no longer told that menstruating women cause flowers to wilt, no longer isolated for the duration, it still lingers in the cultural consciousness that women can pollute, destroy, or dissolve the prevailing structure. The feminine, or the fool, or the angel, then, creates the chaos that shifts the stability of the rigid, hierarchical structures and reveals an order from the deeper realm of story and image—of dream and art.

॰ॐ

The religion with which these pages are concerned is the religion of picking up the pieces, improvising, making up and making do. It is tempting to say that it is the religion of "women and children." It is the religious consciousness that apprehends the sacred without the authority to do so. It is the religion of women, children, and fools. Yet it seems a likely consequence of a culture founded upon iconoclasm as much as dualism, upon the reforming impulses as much as the preserving motivations, upon ordinary experience as much as inklings of transcendence. A dualism that has been secularized is vulnerable to an iconoclasm that is oddly poetic; reformations that have been the stonework in cultural formation carry within themselves their own capacities for explosions of reinterpretation. And all religious institutions, utilizing the stuff of the ordinary transformed into the meaning-complex of the sacred, must bear the possibility of other "stuff" and experience being apprehended as sacred. If a religious tradition decrees a particular day holy, then all other days are potentially holy—or temporally expansive. If a religious tradition decrees a stone holy, then any stone may tell a secret; or if it decrees a story holy, other stories also may conceal themselves in the language, expand the boundaries of knowing. The culture that we know is continually shifting its shape, changing its mind. We currently experience that shift in the realm of our perceptions of women, in the sense of folly, in the aesthetic vision, in the changes in language: these shifts may appear not quite legitimate, but nevertheless they slip into the symbolic consciousness of the dominant culture. Changes in metaphor are changes in religion. The change in religion is the iconoclastic breakdown of the dualistic paradigm and the remythologizing of the world (word) that permits a polyvalent playfulness, a sacralizing of the human experience, an apprehension of the divine in the ordinary.

Iconoclasm is the keynote of the western tradition; yet Abraham's willingness to sacrifice his son (forgoing the image of himself), the breaking of the tablets by Moses (undoing his newly formulated image of order for his own culture, not merely grinding up the sacred bull of his rivals), the *noli me tangere* of Jesus (disrupting his own image), the iconoclasms of all the great reformers and founders—Muhammad, Luther, the monastics, itinerant preachers, are each marked by profound image-making. The western tradition is marked by the dynamic of iconoclasm which is itself a profound image-making or remythologizing of culture. The great iconoclastic impetus in western culture gave rise to prophecy, and prophecy's failure to literalism; its sovereignty was in apocalypticism, and apocalypticism retreated into secular dualism. Woven into all of this, however, is the text-ure of western culture, a metaphorical or imagistic reality.

In the fragmented and haphazard stories we tell, we reveal the shifting and expanding borders of our reality. Stories about family predecessors are sometimes single, sharp images, like odd snapshots: "My grandmother was cutting wood. She chopped off her big toe, stuck it back on and it stayed. I never met her. She died when my mother was three." The woman is remembered or imagined by that single grotesque, if resourceful, act. / "My grandma used to wear her glasses on top of her head and we'd have to look all over the house for them till she found them." / Sometimes they are miniature tales: "My grandpa killed a man and had to swim a river to escape." / "When my grandma was little she didn't know why you shouldn't just lick the iron to see if it was hot instead of licking your finger and then touching the iron." / "My great-grandmother was a poor widow who had a beautiful daughter. There was a handsome man who was going to be in the movies and make lots of money, but the daughter, my grandmother, wouldn't go out with him. So my great-grandmother promised her a new hat if she would go out with him. She went out with him, got the new hat, married him, and he became an alcoholic. He played an old alcoholic in the only movie he was ever in. She divorced him and married a rich manufacturer." / "My mom had trouble spelling 'field' at school. Then she found out she already knew how to spell it because it was at the end of her own name—Scofield."

The stories we tell about our parents and theirs are often fool stories: looking for something that is already part of you, as in "field"; or bribing your daughter to accept a ne'er-do-well for the price of a hat; in the interest of efficiency, suggesting skipping a crucial step in the testing of the hot iron. "When my mother was little, she cut out all of the polka-dots from a rich lady's dress. The rich lady screamed and called her a devil." There is some mysterious way that we affirm ourselves by naming ourselves fool.

Foolishness begins dualistically as that which is opposed to wisdom. The fool loses land and heaven. But the fool's mockery opens up the world, and in the underside, in the seams, in the reflections of our tradition, the fool may become a holy figure, a saint, or even a paradoxical, poetic vision of what it means to be human.

How many people know stories of their great-great-grandparents? Many contemporary people are bereft of any family continuity stories; perhaps that is one of the reasons for the increased interest in tracing family histories, charting ancestries. But information that is available exclusively through oral channels has often evaporated. Shreds of stories remain. To our surprise, many of those great-great-grandparent stories are not about hardships endured, successes, or accomplishments, or wise sayings, but they are the shredded stories of fools. A woman smiles and says,

> My great-great-grandfather had two thumbs on one hand and could pinch. That's pretty funny, two thumbs, when you think [and she pantomimes pounding nails] that he was a carpenter. [She completes her narrative with a summation of an ancestor caricatured.] That's all I know about him: two thumbs on one hand, pinching people, and a carpenter.

Another woman tells all she knows of her great-great-grandmother:

She was a widow, very eccentric, and married a much younger
man. She was in her second childhood, so he got all the land.
It turned out there was oil on it; but he got it.

These examples indicate that the transmission of ancestors is
as likely to be the harboring of fools as the hallowing of heroes.
I suspect this saving of fools is not merely that we have grown
cynical, nor that we recognize that we are not merely the prod-
ucts of our ancestors and thus have no reason to falsely glorify
them; I suspect, rather, that it may be a metaphorical matter:
we need our fool images now, and the stories we must tell on
ourselves are the stories of the fools dangling out of the family
tree.

Even the stories that began as one kind of narrative have
been transformed or remythologized as another. A boy learned
of one distant grandfather who led the Trail of Tears and said
things well worth remembering, such as: "The perpetrator of a
crime never forgives his victims." He learned it, however, from
a book, not from family lore or text-making. He paid little attention to his ancestral hero. In contrast, from one of his great
grandmothers he learned about her grandfather. During the
Civil War her grandfather, then a sixteen-year-old boy, and his
father were Union soldiers cut off from their troop and were
hiding from Rebel forces. The boy's father was caught and
killed, while the youth hid, watching in the bushes, only an arm's
length away. No heroism, no moral, just the story of how a
branch of the family tree was nearly severed before it could
blossom. The boy likes the story about how he himself was almost extinguished long before he was ever born. It's a story no
one ever told his mother; "I knew you wouldn't care about it,"
her grandmother said, "but I figured he would." How did she
know? How do we know which stories to tell our children?
Which stories are ripe?

The stories of fools, of the feminine, stories that riddle or
quest, might slip in and transform a culture that keeps trying
to insist upon the inadequate, dualistic story of combat. Our
dominant culture has represented two inferior images: combat
and consumerism. Kill it or eat it.

The feminine image undermines that dualism; although she

is outside the "masculine" order, and therefore should be kept down, precisely because she is outside, she may find her way around. The parable of the "Doubting Thomist" says,

ↄ

Once there was a man who tried to reach things. "If I am a creature of God," he said, "I should be able to climb up through creation back to God."

"It sounds to me," said his wife, brushing her long wrinkled hair, "like trying to spin straw into gold."

"It sounds like," offered the red-haired child, thinking it was a riddle, "like climbing the beanstalk." He thought riddles were answered by saying quickly the picture that came next.

"It sounds like," added the little child with dark curls, thinking that riddles were no more than everyone having a turn, "God didn't make a ladder yet."

"If only," the man pondered, "I could touch the earth; if I could make contact, truly, with a single object, then I would be able to begin the journey. If I could know a stone, I could enter the stone and ascend back to God."

His wife shelled peas, cracking them open, her thumb forcing them down into the pot in her lap. One of the peas escaped and bounced into the sleeve of her husband. "Try the pea," she said, "keep it under your mattress. Sleep on it."

The red-haired child hooked pea cases on his ears. "I am the giant in the sky," he said, still thinking about the beanstalk.

The littler child held an emptied pod to his lips and wanted to say, "I have giant lips," but his mother kissed him on them instead.

The husband looked with a creased face at the wife; he fumbled for the pea. "This pea," he said, holding it between thumb and finger, "does it exist without its companions, attached by their stems in their pod? If I plant this pea, it will produce more peas. Where is the pea, in the planting or the plant? Does the blossom enfold the eventuality of the pea, and is that eventuality closer to the pea than this little globe?"

"The peas are good this year," his wife responded.

"You're right," the man nodded. "The truth of the pea may be in the taste of the pea. In order to reach the pea, do I need to embrace its entire order—its seasonal, structural, evolutionary orders? Does the pea include the various peas yet to be? I don't know where to begin."

His wife laughed as she always did when he became boring, and lighting a fire, suggested, "Why don't you ask God?"

The children had attached pea pods like clothespins to their tongues, and pretended they were lizards. They repeated the questions of their father as liquid nonsense.

The man, dis-remembering the protocol or procedure involved in contacting the divinities with or without attributes, grumbled, "Why don't you?"

She stared at her husband a long moment. Then she told him to feed the children the peas and the raspberries. She tied a silky ribbon to her hair and went out the door.

"Where are you going?" he called after her.

"To talk with God," she answered over her shoulder. "Did you think that just because I wash scraped knees and embroider grape vines I would want to rub up against God just like that? I need to put something between God and me. I must study; then talk to God."

"Will you be back in time for bed?" he asked.

"Sure," she laughed, and took off running.

The man cried. He blamed God for taking his wife. The children asked where their mother was. He told them she ran off with a gypsy. They looked as though they might have expected to hear it. They ate the raspberries and spilled the peas upon the floor.

The child with the dark curls asked, "Will she come back?"

"Would you want her back after she's been with gypsies?" he asked them sharply.

After it had been moonless dark for a long time, she came back through the door.

The children petted her. They looked at her teeth, her eyes, and felt in her pockets for evidence of gypsies.

The man tried to remember if she had been wearing a ribbon when she left the house.

"Well?" he asked.

"Well."

"Where have you been?"

"To God."

He looked at her teeth, her eyes; he felt in her pockets for evidence. "Did you ask about the pea?"

"The children spilled the peas. God told me."

"What else?" he asked impatiently.

"That's all. There wasn't much time for talk."

She got down on the floor with the children. "God," she told them, fitting pods on her fingers, "likes to make pea-puppets," and showed them. "And fangs," and showed them those.

"We already know how to do those," said the one with red hair.

"I know you do."

Because the man could not believe his wife, he chose no longer to believe in God.

The children didn't believe either, but in their games included God.

☙

The feminine figure, the fool, or the angel tell their stories through the tracing of labyrinths or the telling of riddles, through embroidering grapevines or finding God.

The labyrinth is a persistent figuration in our past, a map of spirituality, a confounding of direction, a symbol of mysteries. Most often, perhaps, we find it disguised as an entertainment, a trivial tribute to our mind. Particularly in botanical labyrinths, mostly grown over since the antimacassars went to the attic, the entertainment alludes to more—to the tensions created between formal, unchanging control and the mysteries of chaos and uncertainty. Created as diversions, elaborate toys, electronic, mechanical, or verbal, they nevertheless cannot fail to trip open the mental passages that trace toward their mythic origins, processional rituals, and at once, to the metaphor of the mind. A religious heritage that sometimes claims one must "keep to the straight and narrow," or "strait is the gate," or "there is one way," is nevertheless honeycombed with labyrinthine alternatives.

Once, in the midst of a peyote ceremony, the Cheyenne singing and chanting suddenly shifted into English, and I heard, "There is only one way, Hay-ya-hay-ya-hay-yay, Jesus is the only way!" The song was a matter of hospitality, honoring the white guests, our friend laughed the next day. I was struck, in that simple labyrinth of the circle, which is so meticulously ritualized in the peyote ceremony, by the sudden intrusion of another metaphorical universe and its exclusivist rhetoric incorporated into an embracing mysticism. Historically, Christianity has itself been effective in incorporating myriads of sacred places, names, patterns, and beings; its cornerstone may be Peter, but its foundation is formed of multicolored, imported stones. Now the secularized labyrinth is named Uncertainty.

The primal labyrinthine garden in our cultural mind is Eden. The maze from which all paths fork, the secret womb from which we struggle to emerge and simultaneously seek the terrible cherubim-guarded door for readmittance. Since the expulsion from the garden, we have been banished to be wanderers in time, and the maze we trace is the channels of time. We pursue the future, which is shadowed by a past, a necessary path our mortal footprints cannot retrace. Our imaginal footprints, however, take us on metaphysical, mystical, or at least amusing, paths. All rivers flow from the imaginary tree in the garden: "A river flowed out of Eden to water the garden, and there it divided and became four rivers." And the waters all evaporate into the mind: "You cannot step into the same river twice."[1] Heraclitus' meaning finally emerged through the modern revision "You can't step into the same river once." The illusion, however, may be in the metaphor of the river. It is not only that the river is constantly changing, or that the persons getting their philosophical feet wet are constantly changing, it is that the metaphorical waters do not follow the same good manners that the waters of nature prefer. The directions----->
---->---> are false maps. Infinity itself maybe a simple line from which there is no escape. "Verily, O Shamash, thy net is the wide earth, Thy snare is the faraway sky."[2] When the paths have been erased (the sacred traditions), but the maps still point (cultural dualism), then the stories will claim, "A cage went in search of a bird,"[3] or

> Through the years, a man peoples a space with images of provinces, kingdoms, mountains, bays, ships, islands, fishes, rooms, tools, stars, horses, and people. Shortly before his death, he discovers that the patient labyrinth of lines traces the image of his own face.[4]

Christian pilgrims tracing their fingers along ecclesiastical labyrinths or scraping their knees along the mazes around the baptismal font, found their ways back to the symbolic city of Jerusalem. Daedalus threaded the seashell and made the minotaur's lair; Ariadne's youths threaded the sacred with ribboned dances. The Cheyenne's trickster, Veheo, bore the same name as the spider, the weaver of snares, the designer of chaos, and the articulator of perfection.

Children spray spiders' webs with sticky paint and attach them to paper, carrying away on paper a mundane secret, an ordinary revelation. The spider starts all over and human beings keep casting back. The labyrinth is language; tracing or erasing the labyrinth is the divine task or game. The sacred box is constructed of trick chambers; we dwell within it. Our capacities for connecting and discriminating, for comparing and transforming, for fabricating (a word that entwines both making and lying) are the labyrinth. Religion cannot, it seems, be metaphorically fashioned into a mere two-sided figure; dualism gives way to other deep images.

Like the labyrinth is the riddle. Dependent, usually, upon paradoxes or puns, riddles (to riddle is to pierce with holes) find the lacunae in ordinary channels of thought and demand that we linguistically undo and remake the world. Through puns and riddles the language copulates; it temporarily gives up discrimination for the sake of integration.

Everyone makes puns. It's one of the primary ways we joke. Before my son was two he was stirring his crumpled papers in a pan with a wooden spoon. "What are you doing?" "I'm making soup," he said solemnly. "What great soup!" I exclaimed. "Yes, it's souperman," he responded soberly. It is not a great pun; but he had not lived long in the realm of language, yet he was turning and overturning categorical possibilities. He was playing. How far is that from sacred language texted always by puns? When Yahweh made a man (*Adam*), he formed him from earth (*adama*). Nabokov has penned, "The pun is mightier than the word." After the flood, in the Greek story, Deucalion and Pyrrha emerged from their ark and in answer to their prayers for the renewal of humanity, the goddess Themis appeared, telling them to throw the bones of their mother behind them. The goddess had given them a riddle, and they deciphered it to mean that their mother was the earth, stones were her bones. They shrouded their heads, threw the stones over their shoulders, and by the process of pun a stone (*laas*) was transformed into a people (*laos*);[5] by the process of riddle the feminine renewed the earth. Jesus said, "And I tell you, you are Peter (*Petros*), and on this rock (*petra*) I will build my church, and the powers of death shall not prevail against it." In the beginning, laid with the foundations, is the generative play of language.

As a child I always liked the comparison of the camel who could more easily pass through the eye of a needle than the rich man could squeeze through the gates of heaven. How disappointed I was to learn at school that the "eye of the needle" may have referred to a particularly narrow gate entering Jerusalem. The mundane comparison turned it back into a mere "teaching story" rather than an absurd, explosive, sacred metaphor. Fortunately, my daughter came home with a horrendous joke: "How do you keep the elephant from slipping through the eye of the needle?" (You tie a knot in his tail.) Somehow the image of contradiction was renewed; the absurdity remythologized the eye of the needle and the pointless childhood joke mingled with the sacred admonition. We perform such riddling tasks constantly, renewing and revitalizing the world we live in. Joyce parodied the Lord's prayer:

> In the name of Annah the allmaziful
> the everliving, the bringer of plurabilities
> Haloed be her Eve
> Her singtime sung, Her rill be run,
> Unhemmed as it is uneven.[6]

and remythologized the feminine, the foolish, the riddling and labyrinthine consciousness.

                              ☙

One can conveniently adjust to or rebelliously combat the world; or one can find the third category of creative, nonconventional integration. I suspect that is why the culture is fermenting so with its fools, women, and angels. These nonheroic, noncombative figures are more likely to marry, tame, play with, pretend to be, or even *be* a dragon than to slay one. The riddling, labyrinthine stories (which do not heroically overcome or conquer the riddle or labyrinth) yield to a more subtle, more playful consciousness. The stories of the feminine and of fools imply more revolutionary, heretical, ecological, erotic, aesthetic, and interior senses of being. Perhaps they are being invoked to revise iconoclastically the prevailing stories, to preside over the remythologizing or cultural shift we are now living.

Our meanderings are multiple, and we can paradoxically seek the rediscovery of the gates of Eden while searching out an escape into a new form. Speculation into the strange is done by retracing the familiar. The labyrinth is a wonderful quest metaphor, which dissolves itself as an object and wrests us from object-thinking. As with the Grail, we are sent on quests with no firm object; the treasure changes form and the quest keeps turning into another map. We, through questing, through riddling, revise our subjects and our objects. The boundaries between become more obscure, and the connections become sharper. In combative models we play rigid games, never forgetting what part we are assigned—never, therefore, making the foolish discoveries of who we are. Questing and quizzing are dangerous, of course; there are man-and-woman-eating plants out there now. And there never were before.

7

The Inward Text
Dream as Scripture

People with no other art forms have three: they can tell their past, they can find humor, and they can recall their dreams.

Long ago, when we said that dreams were sent from gods, the gods themselves seemed to come more frequently to our dreams. But with the dawn of greater self-consciousness—or at least modern consciousness—beings may appear wearing bright green vegetable genitalia and we (with Freudian recall) note the cucumbers, the peaseblossoms, the clover; yet waking from that intimate encounter, we fail to notice that we have been visited by the divine. Since gods are no longer responsible for *sending* our dreams, we no longer recognize them *in* our dreams; what then can dreams have to do with religion?

A dream text says:

> Once Jesus appeared in a dream to comfort me. I thought it was lovely of him to come, considering that I didn't believe in him.

When the gods are not merely literal figures, their sacred habitat is likely to be in dream—one of the few realms left us where time, place, person, and idea can be conflated and configured into maps in which subject-verb-object or space/time are not artificially separated. The dreamer met a Jesus metaphysically transfigured by the ephemeral, and this perhaps at least ephemerally transfigured the dreamer. A Sunday School picture Jesus cannot be counted on for truth or compensation. But in the dream one realizes that the false gods reveal a fragile truth that cannot be verified outside itself; its truth is in the aesthetic or imaginal dimension of our reality.

꒱

Dreams have been suspect in modern culture, rarely mentioned as events worthy of memory or commentary. They are often made up of merely fragments of image: "I went to another planet. It was purple and bubbly. All it had were purply and bubbly books"; or "I laughed so hard my wings rattled. They were metallic and iridescent"; or "I was up on the roof throwing down the junk food characters who advertise hamburgers. I watched them splat"; or "I dreamed the puppy had babies"; "The moon came down and licked a circle round my left breast, lighting it like a candle; then it spun round my other one to fit it like a glowing, lost halo"; or "I was in trouble because I had revived a dead beaver. Everyone was saying, 'Never wake a dead beaver.' "

When dreams were noted in previous times, it was assumed they came from special sources and they were often assigned one of two roles: they were used either as a form of divination or as a means for therapy. It seems that the dream has been recovered in recent times as a religious paradigm (that is, as a comprehensive event which contributes to our reality). The dream has been restored to its sacred sense, not as diviner or healer, but as dream itself.

Balayem, a charming, humorous member of the Tasaday tribe discovered in the Philippines, is reported to have said, "All we know outside our daily life comes from the dreams we have. But we do not know what dreams are."[1] It is difficult, perhaps, to compare ourselves with the gentle Tasaday, a people of almost no material culture, claimed by those who first studied them to have no religion. They do, however, tell stories of the past; they do keep, in a crevice in their cave, heirloom stone tools, finely made models of their own more casually produced ones; they do make jokes; and they do tell their dreams. They are very much like ourselves, in that we too, can say, "All we know outside our daily life comes from the dreams we have. But we do not know what dreams are."

Our western religious heritage has charted an ambivalent attitude toward the dream. The Greeks located the island of Dream between the land of the living and the land of the dead. We glimpse it as Hermes escorts Penelope's dead suitors to Hades, passing by the shores of Dream.[2] According to Hesiod's *Theogony,* Night, the dark and dreadful goddess, "without sleeping with any male," gave birth to her children Destruction, Death, Sleep, Blame, Grief, the Fates, Vengeance, Retribution, Deceit, Old Age, Strife, but also to Love, and certainly to "the race of Dreams."[3] Dreams and Love find themselves siblings to Death, Grief, and Deceit.

These two poems, the *Theogony* and the *Odyssey,* give us Greek mythological origins and location of dreams. And both reveal an ambivalence; the Dream is remote and indistinct, on the peripheries of creation and the cosmos. Dream is between and on the edge; and only in dream can such maps be followed. Dream connects us with those edges of and crevices in reality; and Dream, more than any other of Night's children, has an ambiguous identity, dressing up as all the other siblings, having the theatrical capacity to personify the rest of the family, scripting and memorizing, improvising and plagiarizing from the great documents; Dream writes and performs an Inward Text.

Dream has played two roles with conspicuously traditional religious functions: divination and healing. These two are related and attest to the attempt to make the dream participate in and affect the reality of waking life. Dreams can tell us who we are (divine) or how to become who we are (heal). The divinatory and the therapeutic often rested on the same principles of interpretation; interpretation was an essential aspect of the dream itself. Whenever notice was taken of dream, it was considered almost always to be dependent upon interpretation as part of its being. Therapy and divination, as values in religious institutions, want to get us well, heal us, or put us in harmony. If the dream is understood as primarily aesthetic, the religious consciousness is not toward getting well, but heightening awareness, making the internal a religious function.

Interpretative devices, to judge by those preserved by traditional cultures, were based upon symbolic resonances, whether allegorical or simply associative. The dream was manifested in its interpretation.

An Egyptian dream book from perhaps 2000 B.C.E. lists good dreams in black ink and bad ones in red. The meaning system makes use of verbal and visual resemblances. For instance, the pun: if a man sees his penis stiff, it is a bad dream, meaning victory for his enemies. (*Stiff* and *victory* are explained as punning words.) On the other hand, to see the pun rather than to hear it gives us this interpretation: if a man sees his penis becoming large, it is good, it means his possessions will multiply. Other associations in this system reveal that copulating with his mother is good because it means that his clansmen will cleave fast to him. But to see a woman's pudenda is bad, "the last extremity of misery upon him."[4] As with all systems of interpretation, cultural biases influence the associations.

The symbolic content is linked to daytime prejudices. A sixteenth-century Christian dream interpretation book, attributed to Daniel and dedicated to King Nebuchadnezzar, arranges dream images alphabetically and interprets them like this: "Intercourse with a woman with whom one is acquainted indicates good for all"; but "If you dream of your own wife dancing or leaping, it indicates adultery."[5]

A Blackfeet dreamer, upon waking, would instantly rouse his wife (the old reporters do not tell us of the wives' dreams) and make a speech about it, and then begin to sing, accompanied by his wife. The dream is not the thing that happened in the night but the recollection, the speech, and the song. With important dreams, the experiences were followed by the gathering and fashioning of medicine objects symbolically linked with the dream story.[6]

Reports of dreams in particular cultural contexts often follow conventional "literary" formulas, according to the society and expectations of the dreamers. As dream images are told into the daylight, they take on the dream-ritual or dream-conventions of known dreamers. In some sense it is impossible to dream beyond the "text" of the dreaming experience within a culture. Because the dreams of Joseph can be distinguished from nineteenth-century Plains Indians dreams, we would not accuse these formulaic tale-tellers of deception, but would suggest they were expressing the dreamers' art of their particular culture. Just as the plastic arts can be readily distinguished regarding their cultural origins, so can dreams.

Biblical references to dreams also demonstrate a simple, allegorical understanding of symbol. Indeed, when Joseph dreamed his allegorical and predictive dreams (Genesis 37), his brothers hated him for his dreams and his father rebuked him, "but his father kept the saying in mind." Nevertheless, these dreamers and their texts are generally on the peripheries and in the crevices of their own cultures. Dream interpreters were

> . . . of low standing and often were women. . . . Generally speaking, it can be stated the professional interpreting of dreams seems to have been as rare in Mesopotamia as it was in classical texts and in the Bible. "Symbolic" dreams, and their ingenious and miraculous interpretation, show the most interesting flowering exclusively in literary texts.[7]

The dream has been the source—or what we call a dream—for primary religious revelation; it has been seen as warning, inspiring, healing, predicting, or otherwise interpreting waking life; it has been categorized as a minor, faulty, or demonic form of knowledge, and as a threat to orthodoxy. If we find dream references primarily in ancient literary sources rather than religious ones, why then do we want to call the dream experience "religious"?

The weaving Penelope explained that a dream might come from the Gate of Horn (therefore be valid) or the Gate of Ivory (and be spurious). It is a difficult thing, she suggested, to distinguish between them.

The biblical tradition places dreams below other forms of revelation; although it canonizes Daniel, it also preserves Jeremiah's contemptuous statement, "Let the prophet who has a dream tell the dream, but let him who has my word speak my word faithfully" (Jeremiah 23:28).

> I have heard what the prophets have said who prophesy lies in my name, saying, "I have dreamed, I have dreamed!" How long shall there be lies, and who prophesy the deceit of their own heart, who think to make my people forget my name by their dreams which they tell one another. . . . What has straw in common with wheat? (Jeremiah 23:25–28)

The revelation by dream is suspect. First of all, because we are so easily fooled by those strange images; secondly, I suspect, because the dream, unlike the vision or other extraordinary revelations, comes to all and comes frequently. Orthodoxy itself, or the "truth," is strained unless it can be verified through text or institution. The dream is frequently an affront to the canon, or disappointingly lacking in profundity or coherence. The Greeks had their Asclepian temples; the Christian Gospel of Matthew tells us that Joseph was directed through dream to know that the child conceived by Mary was of the Holy Spirit, and further, to save the child by taking them both to Egypt, where he would finally learn that "those who sought the child's life are dead," and thence return to Israel. Yet the dream is largely ignored or mistrusted.

Perhaps dreams themselves tell us not to trust them. A young man went on a camping trip-quest and had a dream.

> A cosmic sky opened up and the hand of God offered to me a bouquet of grains. Each stalk was a different grain. I was commanded to choose one. I said, "I can't choose. I won't do it." But suddenly and involuntarily I found that I had chosen one. I was holding one of the grains in my own hand. Looking down, I felt relieved that I had chosen the wheat.

The next morning, he reported that he played what he calls "Bible Roulette." Opening the Bible at random, he poked his finger and found a perfect synchronicity in which God spoke and said, "What has straw in common with wheat?" Fortunately or not, he did not bother himself about the context and see that Jeremiah's God was reviling dreamers and those who tell their dreams.

Threatening though dream may be to religious institutions, it was in the move toward secularization and "daylight" consciousness that further dismissal of the dream occurred. We mistrust the image. In the realms of both the sacred and the profane, we have inherited an enormous mistrust of image. And dream is image.

ᶜ'ᴐ

Dream is at once interpretation. Thus it is dangerous, as the traditional story of "The Dream of the Cracked Granary" tells:

> A certain woman came to Rabbi Eliezer and said to him, "I saw in a dream that the granary of my house came open in a crack." He answered, "You will conceive a son." She went away, and that is what happened.
>
> She dreamed again the same dream and told it to Rabbi Eliezer who gave the same interpretation, and that is what happened.
>
> She dreamed the same dream a third time and looked for Rabbi Eliezer. Not finding him, she said to his disciples, "I saw in a dream that the granary of my house came open in a crack."
>
> They answered her, "You will bury your husband." And that is what happened.
>
> Rabbi Eliezer, surprised by the lamentations, inquired what had gone wrong. His disciples told him what had happened. He cried out, "Wretched fools! You have killed that man. Is it not written: 'As he interpreted to us, so it was'? (Gen. 41:13). And Rabbi Yohannan concludes, "Every dream becomes valid only by its interpretation."[8]

Dream, traditionally understood as something to be utilized for divination or therapy, fails to be so compliant when "interpreted." The dream is likely to lie, make us feel bad, or simply be nonsense. The gods no longer hear and the people no longer recall them in their dreams. But the dream is an aesthetic, perhaps our primary aesthetic structure. Rather than look to the other meaning or other being of dream, is it not possible that dream exists for no other purpose than to cast a story, to paint an image on the complexities of existence? The function of dream is aesthetic, not in the sense that it should be turned into art or as an inspiration for artistic production, but in that it is already an aesthetic construct.

Because the dream is aesthetic, it is not merely a repository of misinformation but a primary form of play. It is not a secret codebook for unlocking the mysteries of daylight existence, no matter how the puns unravel our language or the visual shocks reorder our morning perceptions.

Dream disturbs us as it disrupts time. The ancients valued their dreams as passageways for visitations from the ancestors. If contemporary people allow themselves to recall their dreams, those dreams, they find, are often populated by the dead, quickened in the dream world, acting and speaking as though alive, and the death, there, has never occurred. How shall we dream the dead? And how shall our lives be when we waken? One dreamer reflects,

> My grandmother was putting on thick blue and red paint on her face while she talked to me. She insisted that I hug her before I leave and call her when I arrive so she could tell the children I was safe. The embrace I felt in the dream, her body so substantial in the dream, gone to death in wakefulness; her tending to me and the attention to little things of life were the substance of the dream, but in waking they were gone. The thick paint she was putting on seemed so ordinary, casual, in the dream, but so shockingly inappropriate for the plain, straightforward, unpainted grandmother; it disturbed me when I wakened. Was it a death mask I will not accept in my waking? Was the embrace a goodbye I will not acknowledge when I'm awake? In the dream, I feel her, hear her; in the daylight—I feel the melancholy of the loss of her.

Another dreamer said,

> I dreamed of my grandfather. He was sitting in a rocking chair. Other people were sitting behind him in scattered chairs. I was so happy to see him; in the dream itself I said, "I'm so glad he's in my dream because now I can look at his face as

long as I want. I haven't had a chance to see his face like this for years." It was, of course, because he'd been dead for twenty years. I sat on his lap in the rocker and looked at him. He said he came to teach me a game of puns they all knew because he was sure I'd like it. We played a riddle game until I woke.

And the dreamer wakened was riddled for days by the "visitation" of her grandfather and his game. It was, she said, like a gift.

Some dreams among Native Americans, were given as gifts; one could share a dream vision or desire with another person, or give it away absolutely. For instance, if I dreamed of a glorious ice village, I could wish that we might walk together through those glittering trees and visit those charming houses, thus sharing it or giving it as a participatory gift. Or I could give away my dream absolutely. If I dreamed of peaches with jewels inside, I could wish that you should live to receive such fruits. Among the Crow it was once reported that a man dreamed of a very long life. He gave away his dream on a ceremonial occasion to a woman who had given him many things, including horses. The story claims that the man died soon after he bestowed his gift, and the woman lived a very long time.

c·つ

There are several immediate claims against the dream as art form. Each has its limitations, however. The first is the *utter privacy* of the dream. Perhaps the most universal element of the dream is, paradoxically, its unique and nontransmittable qualities. Or, as Heraclitus said, "The waking have one world in common; sleepers have each a private world of his own."[9] The inviolable space of the dream cannot be transgressed by another. Perhaps, even in this age of individuality, or of communal selfishness, we are embarrassed by something so personal and ask can it be worth anything if it cannot be shared? This intimate art, where artist and patron are one, in which the dream symbol, though more than code for neurotic responses to one's personal life, or code for analogues to transpersonal symbol, is woven of the connections to waking life and to universal literature. As an unrepeatable constellation among the universal, cultural, and personal aspects of imagery, the dream is an art form for one. The dream is not so much symbolic analogue to the "collective unconscious" as it is evidence for "the poetic basis of mind." [10]

But among any of the arts, only a portion of the intent is transmitted. Another hearing or seeing creates another configuration of context and content. The dream is more obviously constructed by memory out of remembered unconscious experience, and the dreamer knows there are gaps. These lacunae haunt dreammakers like empty frames witnessing to stolen paintings cut from them, yet since waking memory plays its part in the formation of the dream text, the choices made by memory really create the dream. The artist does not paint everything seen; the filmmaker edits; art is made by leaving out, by selecting. The first issue, that of privacy, is countered by the elements of symbol that can be shared; moreover, it is overcome by the acceptance of dreamer as audience as well as player. Works and plays do not have to be produced on a public stage; intent can be esoteric. Dream is, perhaps, the most esoteric and simultaneously the most universal of our arts. A dream that recalls the conventions of Restoration comedy maintains the utter privacy of the sleep theatre:

> I was in a Restoration comedy. I sat at an ornate desk dressed in velvets and laces. Beside me was a large easel. With a plume in one hand, a paintbrush in the other, I simultaneously wrote at the desk and painted at the easel. Suddenly from stage left rushed a dragon. I stopped him with a gesture of my brush, and proclaimed, "Some people find that they prefer ham and eggs to eggs existential."

Yet it is not necessary to know that the dreamer had been irritated by fraudulent philosophers; the flimsy art of the dream rests upon the silly word play that tells the same story.

Dreams are among the ephemera of our lives that, like a child's box under the bed, open up religious consciousness. They do not tell truths, or explain the world, or make us better people; they play upon the themes that make us human.

A three-year-old woke from her nap and excitedly told her dream. It seemed to be the first time she fully understood the difference between waking and dreaming. She had reached a level of consciousness that could separate "reality" from "fantasy."

> I dreamed my dolls were really babies. They were really alive babies.

At the same time, she had come to experience the symbolic, which synthesizes a world discriminated. She knew her dolls were inanimate objects, and she knew, through them, the feeling for "really alive babies." The dream was not merely an empty fantasy, but a rich encounter.

The second issue that militates against our acceptance of dream as aesthetic consciousness is its *incoherent* form. Part of the reason it cannot be transmitted is that it cannot be translated. But just as we would not presume that a novel could be translated into a film, or that anyone ever could really tell us all about that great film they saw last night, we know that another person can never thoroughly or authentically experience someone else's dream. A dream cast into another form in order to repeat or evoke the dream experience becomes the dream experience, just as a film based upon a novel becomes a film, not a translated novel.

But in dwelling on the untranslatable quality of dream, we can ignore that dreams do translate into other realms. And dreams are already translations or unravelings of the ordinary. A dreamer was in a wheelbarrow, hurtling toward the fiery mouth of hell. When had she heard the cliché "going to hell in a handcart"? Another dreamer stuck to the walls of her room while people came in and out, looking at her. She maneuvered the walls like an insect. Even in the daylight she had been "climbing the walls." A boy was stuck inside a ladybug; in the daytime he had been told that the beetles (Volkswagens) were too small. A woman dreamed of beautiful, iridescent, floating creatures, something like fish, but floating in the air, waving their exotic plumes. They were, I suppose, "neither fish nor fowl."

Our clichés are folk art, developments of powerful, apt metaphors worn smooth of the images that generated them; dreams take them up and transmute them. One dreamer was particularly disturbed that she saw people walking around who had giant hands instead of heads. She tried to get away from them because they were grotesque. Later the next day, the dream nudged her until she came upon the word "handicapped." Another dreamer found himself walking around in his father's shoes. The puns inherent in a word made their way into this dream:

> There were hills, trees, and garden walks. No one knew the way. I was among those going on the pathway, and then I was apart. I became the guide; they made their ways through the labyrinth toward me. I stood on the stone steps of the Temple. They finally came to the end of the maze where I was. I slowly repeated, round and round, my message. They must understand; but I did not know if they did: "Naut-the-astro—naut-the-astro—naut-the-astro," over and over. I thought it was really profound until I was completely awake.

The dreamer wound through the maze of a simple word, astronaut, binding that search back to the labyrinth of earth and earthlings. The puns in these dreams, or the transliterations of the pictures hiding in our language, are not the dreams, not the interpretations of the dreams, nor their meanings. They are part of that dream art, the aesthetic base of our reality. The dreaming mind appreciates pun as does the numinous consciousness. Ancient religious literature abounds in puns as sacred language. A pun is a magical device for turning one thing into two, or three into one. It is the essence of symbol; it is the stuff dreams are made on.

The third problem in understanding dream as aesthetic structure comes from the notion that our dreams come to us *unwilled,* unbidden. We have no control; we are not really the creators. It helps us, anyway, not to accept the guilt, the darkness, and the chaos that dream seems to force upon us. Or even the more pleasant gifts of dreams seem to be unworthy because they were unearned.

The gifts that dreams usually give us, however, resemble the secrets earned in religious ceremonies—they have no value outside of the context. My son once dreamed that he went into a cave, seeking a great treasure. He found an old man who said he had gotten rid of the treasure, but he gave him some junk he liked. In another dream he sought the lion. He opened the door, found a chest, opened it up, and took out . . . an ice cream cone—as the great mysteries within the boxes of the world's religions, whenever they are uncovered by others from other worldviews or contexts, seem pitifully inadequate. The mysteries of the great religions cannot be reduced to "wish-fulfillment," so perhaps we can look more closely at the powerful gum-ball machines, flying horses, and talking trees of children's dreams, too, as the imaginal work/play of human consciousness. A dreamer dreamed:

> My husband was sending our friend and me back to school. I said we'd better look in the sky because there were lots of stars to see. The sky was very black. A white light streamed across the night. It was a great flying horse. I said smugly, "I know what it really is. It's on the side of a blimp that you can't see." "No," he answered, "this is the real one. Pegasus." I called the horse closer to us, to prove whatever the nature of his existence. He swept down to us, hovering in the air, and I could see that he was made of huge sheets of white typing paper. He was larger than a flesh-and-blood horse, fully modeled, but made of glued-together giant typing paper. He was edged with little rows of glitter, reminding me of how stingy the teachers used to be when they dispensed the glitter. I wanted my husband to see him, and sent him to the upstairs bedroom window. "Look," I said. "The flying horse has escaped from a pageant from the sixteenth century. They were making him for a processional." My husband got the children and we decided to follow the horse back down the road to see the sixteenth century up close.
>
> The people's faces were fascinating, out of old paintings. I went into a little secondhand store and was going to purchase an old, used beaded purse; it was a wonderful chance to bring

back something through time. "Won't people be surprised," I
told the children, "to see that Victorian beaded purses were
modeled on sixteenth-century ones we didn't even know
about." I was careful to choose one intact. Some of them had
things in them. I looked, and found they were nothing but
extra beads. I got one with beads inside.

Then everyone was rushing to a church. We went along. I
was sad to see it was a funeral mass. A child was in a glass
coffin along the side of the church, not near the priest. The
parents came in weeping. Three, very small, cheerful-look-
ing, little old ladies came in; I think they used to run a book
store. One of them went to the coffin and smiled at the child.
He stirred. She saw me watching closely and smiled at him
again. I thought, the baby looks as if it is coming back to life;
but it can't. If it would wave its arms I would believe it. He
waved his arms. He was about a year-and-a-half old, plump
and beautiful. I thought, it's so difficult to tell the difference
between death and life. The little old woman smiled and nodded to him again. I thought, if he would sit up I would believe it. He sat up and rubbed his eyes, looked around, like
a child waking from a nap. The parents cried and rushed to
gather him up and ran with him out of the church. How easy
this is, I thought, now we'll be able to do it any time we want.
We just have to think.

She does not acknowledge the doctrine of resurrection any
more than she accepts the literal existence of winged horses;
but she carried the dream into her daylight, just as within the
dream she carried an old "used" beaded purse, containing
nothing more than beads, as her treasure from the sixteenth
century. Purses and dreams are "boxes." The transformations
of time, of paper horses and tiny old women, of stillness into
life, is figured in fraying purses and worthless dreams. Just as
the beaded purse contains nothing more than loose beads, the
dream structure carries nothing more than "loose" images.
Treasures are not literal; dreams are religion.

In seeking ourselves in our dreams we can be mistaken into
seeking meanings. It is the error of all the world's dreamers,
but not of the dreams themselves. My son dreamed that he was
playing in the laundry room while I did the wash; he discov-

ered a big bag of coins. "You can save them in your room," I said in the dream. "No," he tells me he explained, "there's no use; because these are not real coins because this is just a dream." Once we discover repeated images and connections between images, along with the concomitant feelings, we sometimes mistake the images themselves for "archetypes" or "meanings" or desire to spend dream coins in our daylight contexts; they are currency for the imaginal, religious realm. The dream relies upon correspondences, in the places between, not upon objects. Dreams are not logical but mytho-logical; they sew terror and absurdity together; they disintegrate the dreamer. The art form of the dream, like play, like little saved things, like memory, is to make a human life, to participate in the making of human culture.

There are, of course, famous dreams that have inspired great inventions or artistic productions. The aesthetic form of our dreams in this context, however, does not refer to the benzine ring, the Indian goddess who visited the mathematical genius in his dreams, or Coleridge and his "Kubla Khan." Even if Coleridge dreamed his poem, it was the life of the poet that made possible the dream. Most dream poems, dream ideas, or dream paintings pale before the critical, daylight eye. Since we have not formed our aesthetic theories for the art of dream, we apply the wrong standards to dream works. A dream was reported of an apocalyptic vision of a burning, seething landscape with floating objects decaying in a murky body of water, accompanied by this "poem":

> The bones stuck through the earth's crisp crust.
> Pickles floated in a brine.
> We thought the earth would end in dust.
> So this must be only a sign.

As a poem it is really rotten; as dreamer's art it may be thoroughly compelling.

We mistrust the dream too because it seems *unrepeatable*. It is a text that cannot be translated or even recalled. Most dreams, even if remembered or recorded, get cold, lose their impact, dry up. It is a transitory art form. The saturation of meaning and nuance of feeling from which a dream was born may dissipate with the weeks, except for a few, which seem to persist in populating daylight awareness and have come to stay. Transitory arts, those which are eaten or washed away, the spontaneous joke or the profound moment between two people, can be as significant as monuments, though their significance is not of the same sort as the monumental. Even the dreams we save are saved like old letters.

My son dreamed one night:

> We found a secret place in the house. Behind the wall were many caskets. Dad went back there and was dragging the caskets out into the house. Mom was pissed off and said, "Put them back." Dad kept bringing them out. Finally he brought out a really old one. We opened it up. There was Grant. Mom screamed, "Then who the hell is buried in Grant's tomb?"

Classic dream art.

ᴄ·ᴐ

Dream is text. Text, etymologically, is weaving. And so we turn to the dreamer, that is, to the weaver.

Nick Bottom, in *A Midsummer Night's Dream,* is a weaver and aspiring actor who desires to play every part. It is not enough for him to be offered the part of the sweet-faced, tragic hero, Pyramus. He could move us to storms of tears as Pyramus the lover, he claims; but he could also play a ferocious tyrant. "Let me play the lion, too. I will roar, that I will make the duke say, 'Let him roar again, let him roar again.'" Bottom knows what all dreamers know, that one must play all the parts.

In fear of frightening their audience so much that the actors might risk being hanged, Bottom promises to roar "as gently as a sucking dove." The dove and the lion conflate in his patchwork mind like a dream.

Assigned the role of the sweet-faced man, Bottom promises to rehearse most "obscenely." He means "seemly," of course; but as in dream he dramatizes and unconsciously puns. Through error he makes his language richer and more precise. Nick Bottom mingles seemly and obscenely. Perhaps "obscene" refers obliquely to what is offstage, out of the scene, the place where Bottom's Will shapes his sphere.

For fear of frightening the ladies with their "disfigurations" the actors promise a prologue, explaining away killings and lions. The motivation for the prologue is to prevent us from mistakenly asking that this "play" be divinatory (literalized) or therapeutic (having the power to kill or cure). Yet precisely because it does resonate with the outer play, it is divinatory; and precisely because it cannot kill or cure, it is able to plunge Bottom to his depths, as well as to the limits of his fragile, fumbling wit. He even solves the problem of the wall. Like a dreamer, he knows that the wall, too, is a character. "Some man or other must present Wall." Bottom, the dreamer, knows that dreamers play all of the parts in their dreams, from Moonshine to Lion, from Fair Ladies in the Audience to Wall.

Bottom becomes more than weaver and more than play-maker; he becomes enchanted, and, under enchantment, though wearing an ass's head, he becomes erotically entangled with the queen of the fairies. Dreamers play out the erotic with fools like Don Quixote or Santa Claus as a yogic master. Bottom is beloved of Titania, the fairy queen; they sleep, embracing; but Bottom awakens alone, "with his own fool's eyes peep." He awakens seeking his cue for his "merry tragedy," and says,

> I have had a most rare vision. I have had a dream, past the wit of man to say what dream it was. Man is but an ass, if he go about to expound this dream. Methought I was—there is no man can tell what. Methought I was—and methought I had—but man is but a patched fool if he will offer to say what methought I had. The eye of man hath not heard, the ear of man hath not seen, man's hand is not able to taste, his tongue to conceive, nor his heart to report, what my dream was. I will get Peter Quince to write a ballet of this dream. It shall be called "Bottom's Dream" because it hath no bottom; and I will sing it in the latter end of a play, before the duke. Peradventure to make it the more gracious, I shall sing it at her death. (Act IV, Scene 1)

Confusing, distorting, and burlesquing I Corinthians, "Eye hath not seen, nor ear heard, neither have entered into the heart of man the things which God hath prepared for them that love Him," the dream text is woven of tangles of other texts, sacred and ordinary. Bottom tangles scripture and Peter Quince's ballet, as yet unwritten. Only an ass would expound such a dream; but only a mortal such as Bottom would meet with fairies. His encounter with fairies seems ordinary until he sleeps—and wakes—and counts his contact as a dream. He makes it art and calls it "Bottom's Dream."

Artemidorus' Dream Book interprets the dream image of wearing asses' ears: "To have asses' ears is a good omen only for a philosopher because the ass will not listen and give in easily. To all other people it means servitude and misery."[11] For Bottom, the experience of asses' ears must have marked him as a philosopher. As a weaving philosopher, he threads his way back to Heraclitus, the pre-Socratic philosopher, who said, "You could not discover the limits of soul, even if you traveled every road to do so; such is the depth of its meaning." The soul, like Bottom's dream, "hath no bottom." It must then be expressed by fools and philosophers. It must be played and imagined. Bottom had Heraclitus call us back to remember what it is that dreams and "such stuff as dreams are made on" have to do with religion. Dreams locate our lives in a metaphorical understanding of experience, in the symbolic quality of non-causal connections that weave the fabric of our texts. Living in a secularized context, a place with iconoclastically decaying myth, we will be imagined out of the bottomless, foolish stories we tell ourselves.

8

The Make-Believe of Belief Deliteralizing and Remythologizing

The new idea, the original event, is a celebration of the ignorance of past and future. It is the mask of iconoclasm.

Iconoclasm is a fundamental impulse in the western tradition; it is the impulse for purifying, revitalizing, strengthening, rescuing a decaying tradition. It is the impulse for freeing ourselves from an old bondage. The iconoclasm of our time, however, may paradoxically resemble or reassemble the old myths. To tell a story in our time iconoclastically deconstructs the dualistic heritage. Perhaps the contemporary iconoclastic impulse is no longer the work of demythologizing but of remythologizing. Through iconoclasm, breaking down the dualistic structure of the old order, we can rediscover among the rubble, as children do, the stuff for our boxes, the phrases for our texts, the residues of our dreams. It is work that is play, it is a means of finding the creatures that have disappeared. It is not a simpleminded matter of leaving behind technology, history, or secular culture; it is a matter of perceiving them as

mythic constructs. Moreover, it is a matter of perceiving ourselves mythically. That is not to suggest that we can take on
paper-doll characteristics of so-called archetypes, but that we
call upon the transcendent which gives birth to the particular
in our lives. It means that prevailing metaphors shift. We are
living through a paradigm shift; the prevailing metaphors are
metamorphosing. As our images shift their shapes, we change
our minds, and our universe trembles.

༂

The most fundamental or transformative events can come in
the smallest images. Sometimes they expand the universe, other
times they diminish its boundaries. A man recalled his earliest
impression of the word "religion": "I was swinging my older
sister's necklace over my head. I didn't know it was a rosary. I
had meant to tease my sister, but she told me to stop because I
was angering God." The beads took on a strange interest, but
religion seemed as repellent as the power a big sister has over
a little boy. Instead of mythologizing the world through such
an event, the child became interested in demythologizing a capricious power and left behind the god who was on his sister's
side. A woman remembered, "A preacher said that angels don't
really have wings. It's silly and childish to think of them with
wings." The attempt to clip the angel's wings, grounding the
concept by removing its imagistic source, is a pale version of
demythologizing. "I worried," she said, "what angels did if they
couldn't fly." Without playfulness, the woman saw no reason to
admit angels at all. There was a man who walked city streets all
his life and collected playing cards that he found lying on side-
walks, odd cards here and there through the years. Eventually
he had acquired a full deck—including the joker—but when he
died, his wife threw them out as litter, not having perceived
them as a text of a man's solitary walks through the years. The
profound ways in which we can misunderstand one another are
charted in the various directions we might be taking in our ex-
plorations of the inner world. There is a form of demythologizing that does not enhance mature development but simply

inhibits the essential human quality of metaphorical vision. The task for the contemporary mind is to deliteralize, and to re-mythologize.

Views of the universe are views of the self. The world can be expanding, contracting, dying, changing; the universe itself can be understood as curious, conscious, telling its own story, bound into cycles or expanding into spirals; the cosmic can be comic, mirroring society, or society can be the illusion of the cosmos; it can be mythically perceived as aesthetic, mechanical, organic, or as thought itself, limitless or bounded, ephemeral or eternal. Whatever *in* the universe is created, consumed, or conjured, *is* the universe.

Now that we have learned that the true feathers from the wings of the Holy Ghost might have been plucked from a domestic fowl, that all religious heroes have suspicious circumstances surrounding their births, that the magicians of the past would be mere charlatans today, then what stories will be told? Stories of charlatans.

༄

"Magic is the means to an endlessness," he winked; the shells overtook the after-images of one another.

"Are you a charlatan?" the little boy asked, slipping away from his mother's grasp.

"Try me," he said, pointing long fingers at the walnut shells. The middle one leapt like a jumping bean.

The little boy shrewdly tapped the one to its left. The magician lifted the cup and revealed a miniature gold coin. "I won!" screamed the boy and grabbed the tiny coin.

"Now am I a charlatan?" the magus asked. "You have a genuine gold coin for my proof."

"You're true and real," said the boy, looking from the giver to the gift.

"Then look here," said the man, grinning; and the boy went white with doubt as the magician's hand overturned the shell on the right. It revealed a live toad.

"I did win. I guessed right!" exulted the boy. The toad, about to leap, was stopped by the long fingernail of the juggler; and the toad turned to emerald. The man looked at the boy, who stared at the emerald, larger, greater by far than the small gold coin in his palm.

"It isn't real. It's really only a toad," protested the boy. "I chose right."

"It's easier to believe in a toad that isn't here than an emerald that is," said the man. "Easier still, that a coin in your hand is more valuable than an emerald less than an arm's length away." The boy did not answer. "But what about the middle cup? It seemed to jump," suggested the magician.

"There wouldn't be anything there," said the boy. "You were trying to trick me into choosing it."

"Trade!" challenged the man. "Trade me that small coin for whatever crouches here."

"No," said the boy and ran away into the crowd. Without hesitation another little boy stepped into the dust where the first had departed. "Show us," he whispered, gesturing toward the shell. It seemed to the new boy that the shell was levitated the width of a blade of grass.

"What do you have to trade?" asked the man, eyeing the little boy's long afternoon shadow.

"I have my apprenticeship to you," announced the child. The man looked long at the boy and seemed about to cry.

"I have nothing to teach. I am a charlatan," he confessed.

"How did the shell leap by itself?" protested the boy.

"I don't know," wept the magician. "I never know what will turn up." To prove it he spread out his hands and seven more shells slid onto the table. He twisted them into many patterns, then slowly overturned them, one at a time, revealing in turn: a moth, a drop of blood, three that held nothing at all, a signet ring, and the last, again, held nothing.

"But," said the boy, "you are trying to trick me. You are trying to make me forget about the one that jumped. You haven't turned it over yet. Let me."

"No," said the man. "That one is for me."

"But you offered it to the other boy."

"Offering what will not be accepted is keeping for oneself."

"How could you know it would not be chosen? How can you know it will not be chosen if you claim that you don't know what's under it?"

"I am a charlatan. The ones for me are hidden from me." The man's hand trembled as he reached to turn over the shell.

He lifted it and there was a little green, hard pea. "I guessed right," he sighed. "I never know myself where it will turn up."

"I could work weekends," said the little boy.

The great traditions have never claimed that they would uncover anything greater than a pea: Jacob used a stone for a pillow and dreamed of the angels ascending and descending; Chuang Tzu found a butcher who never had to sharpen his knives because he cut only in the places between, the places where there is nothing; Julian held an imaginary hazelnut in her hand and recovered the sufferings of Christ; the charlatan uncovered gold coins, emeralds, moths, blood, rings, nothing, and the little green, hard pea.

Reports of mystical experiences frequently suggest that the profound event was based upon "nothing much." There is a report of a childhood experience that indicates one of the ways in which the ephemeral or the fragmentary might impinge upon the mystical:

> I went into the woods, following my Spring feelings for a new kind of aloneness. Without yet breasts, blood, reason or want—I came into my whole self, into God, into One.
>
> From the gritty road, leaping over the blackberry ditch, I was transposed into filtered light and cushioned forest. Freed into this enclosure—warmer, colder than my mother's house—the narcotic scent of the forest made the top of my head sparkle light, and way inside me warm and heavy.
>
> There in the shade was a tiny, luminous blossom. A yellow violet. I had only known purple violets. My mother's voice whispered, "Johnny Jump-Up." A yellow violet. The wallpaper in my room my mother had picked and put up was garlanded round with violets. My yellow room had purple flowers. How many times my eye had traced the flat petals. First the big wide one at the bottom. The one at the top nearly split like a heart. And the two narrow ones emerge from the sides. Count four or five? Numbers wouldn't separate. Little black lines and powdery center. This has five. Dogwoods have

four; blood-tinged cross, crown of thorns. My grandmother chewed their twigs on her way to school—my size once, me now. My mother's eyes are violets, her hair yellow; her mind knows, originates in this place. I touch her voluptuous, kitchen-aroma'd body held round in violet-patterned cotton. All scents mingle—my mother, the new wallpaper, this place, my grandfather's cedar trees. Between my giant grandfather's big trees and his narrow house are the purpl'd yellow'd pansies. They are unshy violets with fierce faces. Pansies love; the more you pick them the more they grow. Unplucked their terrible scowls won't come. What uncanny knowledge edged in the velvet, furry faces that I feel, far from my grandfather's house.

Purple—yellow—countered my mind, opposite, same, transformation. This flower, my giant grandfather. Everything connected to everything else. All my existence called up meanings. This miniature plant of manifold meanings, generating manifold images on each, infinitely . . .

My mind spiraled; I looked up through a spider web, through fir boughs, through clouds, the subtle shadows spun mauve, golden, gray.

I went away. Forever. When I returned I touched the flower's soft face, slid my finger down the slender stem that had forced its form. I followed that energy back through nature and time to the source—and found myself touching the blossom now.

And I knew everything, and it had nothing to do with feeling, form, or flower. It had nothing to do with my mother— and I never told her.

Whether her experience originated from the divine or from faulty chemistry is not at issue; the transformative experience creates a consciousness that in turn forms all subsequent experience. It is what is called metaphor.

Even if the divine is understood as utterly transcendent, the divine confronts the human from within the human voice and vision. As Eckhart said, "The eye by which I see God is the same eye by which God sees me: one in seeing, one in knowing, one in loving." Eckhart, of course, was one of the great mystics. What about the "secular" person who seeks or perceives no transcendent? The primary experience, no matter how it is interpreted, seems to be inherent in the human capacity for symbol-making. A father draws the solar system on the back of an envelope, noting which planets are too cold, too hot, and why. The child learns the rudimentary map of our system, while the father is fleetingly reconnected to the macrocosm-microcosm metaphor that our civilization outgrew four centuries ago. A woman too sophisticated to take angels literally, or even to pay attention to their metaphorical tradition, suddenly comes upon a charred newspaper that resembles a wing and, for a moment, thinks of angels.

ᕲ

Visiting some friends on the Northern Cheyenne reservation, I watched the woman's beautiful brown arms, adorned in turquoise and silver, making order in the form of a stack of fried bread, while the man entertained us, honoring his guests with his eloquence. Insects followed the children, invading and swarming patterns that mocked chaos. Up near the ceiling, hidden behind other things crowding a narrow shelf, the man removed a small photograph. It was bent, much handled, very precious, a picture of himself and a woman dressed up in "authentic" Plains Indians costumes as they appeared on a movie set. Such heirloom clothing had mostly disappeared from the reservation, sold to outside collectors; and to see themselves as "Indians" required makeup and play. In some sense we are all captives of a reservation culture, our heirlooms lost, our only claim consumerism.

The means that we have available to make ourselves and mark that making are as varied as making bread, telling stories, saving something on a high shelf. To mislay or discard all "pictures" of ourselves is to be, not without mere heirlooms, but without religion—the connecting, authenticating principle of human existence. However, intentionally to turn away from or to deface familiar images of ourselves is a creative and even a religious act. Marking out is still marking; a time of disruption, or of iconoclasm, is a time of transformation. On that high shelf, or in a box, behind the clutter, is a picture; what will we be able to see in it, reinterpreting and reimagining those old visions?

Behind our ethics are images; preceding ethical consciousness is metaphorical consciousness; behind the laws are the stories. Behind the law: "When a stranger sojourns with you in your land, you shall not do him wrong. The stranger who sojourns with you shall be to you as the native among you, and you shall love him as yourself" is the image: "for you were strangers in the land of Egypt." The Hebrew concern for the stranger is bound up in the Hebrews' "photograph" of themselves as wanderers. Unless we look behind our ethical premises to the images that are their foundations, we cannot develop within our ethical realm, or within its foundation, poetic consciousness.

Having forgotten or rejected the traditional texts, we must fabricate, make up our sacred stories as we go along. If the traditional story of the Fall now reverberates with dualism and its sexist and anti-ecological subcategories, and yet our personal memories keep insinuating the same old images even though we have neglected the old story, what shall we do? Medieval travelers tried, by means of geography, theology, and imagination, to find their way back to Paradise. The contemporary imagination no longer seeks that prelapsarian womb; if we make the journey to Paradise, we want to look over its walls and glimpse the Garden after the Fall:

༄

Is the Garden overrun with weeds?

Does God himself tend the Garden now that the expulsion of his farmer leaves it to tangle and leaves it to run back to chaos?

Is the Angel who guards the Gates of the jungle-it-has-become snatching an overhanging, overripe pear or pomegranate, wiping the juice on his sleeve, and searing the surroundings with his glance, looking for interlopers? If we cannot quite see what has become of Paradise, we can see that the surrounding land is all barren from the intensity of the piercing, searching gaze in the Angel's history of watch.

Now and then God wishes to walk up and down in the Garden in the cool of the evening, as in the Good Old Days, reminiscing about the youth of eternity, feeling the little Serpents slide out of his pathway.

God trips on tangled vines and gnarled, exposed roots, almost Falling himself. The undulations of the Serpents wave the tassles of seeded grass like flags of truce.

He steps with his bare feet into rotted fruit on the Garden floor and dissipates once more into the air, memory unfulfilled, queasy again at his creation.

The Angel looks at the shimmering spaces where God no longer appears, smiles, and queries, "What has God rot?"

There is another Punishment.

God sends the Angel falling in a curving arc; and God himself guards the Gates. The Angel, banished from the doorway to Eden, is plunged to deeper passages and portals.

Now how will anyone walk in the Garden? The little Serpents massage their bellies on the wrinkled pits and slip through the slime of the fruit spilled by the Tree.

God looks at the Fallen fruit and muses, "It's a little spoiled, a little overrun, but still Winter hasn't dared to creep in under my gaze. Perhaps it's salvageable."

And the ideas of salvation and winter, rebirth and dying, again sneaked through the Gates of Eden through the mind of God.

Deep in the Garden, though, the little Serpents were pointing the directions with quicksilver tongues, grazing the magenta-tipped, brown-spotted leaves, making loopy hollows under the earth, spaces in the shapes of their wingless, legless bodies.

Looking toward a long night, they sang to one another, "Once God imagines something, it manages to sneak in past him."

Another little Snake said, "Winter and salvation for Eden, imagined in one divine breath."

"How," another asked slyly, "when we slip back out of hibernation, will we be able to tell whether we are in the Garden or out of it?"

A long, old Serpent, dripping out of a Tree from above, suggested, "But the fruit had been rotting already."

And the little Serpents all curved round and asked, "Who could have thought it?"

God turned his gaze from the Garden toward the desert.
"I want to remember how it was that I imagined the Fall when
I meant, I think, to make Eden never Winter."

Another little Serpent said, "If God has begun to watch the
Gates himself, he's imagining someone trying to get through.
They'll get through the same way. He's already let them past
by thinking it possible, or necessary to prevent."

"What shall we do to welcome their arrival?" smiled the
Serpents to God.

⌒

The new arrivals in the Fallen Eden will make myths to ac-
count for History, the myth of demythologizing. They will
laugh and know, too, that they will die. They will do no more,
perhaps, than all of us do, caught in those moments that transcend themselves precisely because they make no more than
their ephemeral, transitory claim.

My wedding dress was satin, sewn with seed pearls on the
bodice, with tapered sleeves, with yards of skirt. While I was
away studying the Comedies, my mother had made it to fit me
precisely from her perfect memory of my body still curled inside her. She made only one error on the dress: she pricked
her finger with the needle and a miniscule drop of blood stained
the waist. No one would see it. My mother was peculiarly
pleased, and she said to me over and over, "Oh well, no one
will see it—and," laughing lightly, "it's got my life blood on it."

My mother was not aware of the fairy-tale motif the Grimms
gathered nearly two centuries ago, of the mother who sent her
daughter off on a journey. To seal her safety, the mother gave
her daughter the only amulet available to her: she pricked her
finger and stained a pure white handkerchief with three drops
of her own red blood. Even if we do not recall the stories, we
will make them.

Through remythologizing, or entering the imaginal, one
transforms time and space. They are not lost, denied, or dis-
torted; but they become qualities rather than quantities. Whatever it is that we do or undo, think or forget, we are participating in the creation of the universe. In making ourselves we

make the universe. In making ourselves, we make the universe, just as Richard of St. Victor made his "box."

Following Richard of St. Victor, the unknown fourteenth-century author of *The Cloud of Unknowing* evokes the memory of the Ark of the Covenant. The box maintained its holy power because part of its story was that it was lost, that it disappeared. Thus it was easy for the *Cloud*'s author to compare the grace of contemplation to the "prefigured" Ark. "For just as in that ark all the jewels and relics of the Temple were contained, in the same way in this little love, when it is offered, are contained all the virtues of a man's soul, which is the spiritual temple of God."

The progress of contemplation was threefold in the *Cloud:* first, Moses, who had to climb the mountain with great effort and was seldom permitted by God to see the Ark; second, "Beseleel, who could not see the Ark before he had fashioned it with his own skill, helped by the pattern that was revealed to Moses on the mountain"; and third, Aaron, who had the Ark in his keeping and could touch and see it whenever he liked.

One is tempted to warp and distort the analogy of the tenders of the Ark in the *Cloud* to say: since the Temple is destroyed (or, as a friend of mine likes to say, "de-storyed"), none of us can part the veil and see and touch the ark whenever we like; and since none of us has been invited to climb the mountain or had the mists at the top parted, then it has fallen upon us to be as Bezaleel, to form the Ark with our own hands—to make our own metaphors from such shards of stories ("the pattern that was revealed . . .") as we have.

The "box" has a false bottom in it, where rings are hidden, where ladies appear to be sawn in half, where gods leave their memories like shed skins.

Notes

CHAPTER 1

1. Patrick J. Geary, *Eurta Sacra: Thefts of Relics in the Central Middle Ages* (Princeton, New Jersey: Princeton University Press, 1978), p. 31, (ref. MGH Epist. v, p. 363; PL cxvi, col. 77).

2. This point is made by various scholars and very effectively by Wilfred Cantwell Smith, in *The Meaning and End of Religion* (New York: Harper & Row, Publishers, 1978, first pub. 1962), pp. 17–19, and entire discussion. Particularly relevant, as well, is his essay, "Secularity and the History of Religion," in *The Spirit and Power of Christian Secularity,* ed. Albert Schlitzer (Notre Dame, Indiana: University of Notre Dame Press, 1969), pp. 33–58.

3. Franz Kafka, *The Great Wall of China,* trans. Willa and Edwin Muir (New York: Schocken Books, 1970), Reflection #17, p. 165.

4. *Richard of St. Victor: The Twelve Patriarchs, The Mystical Ark, Book Three of the Trinity,* trans. and intro. Grover A. Zinn, Classics of Western Spirituality (New York: Paulist Press, 1979).

5. Ibid., p. 366.

6. Ibid., p. 34.

7. Sir James Frazer, *The Golden Bough,* Volume XI (New York: St. Martin's Press, 1966, orig. pub. 1913) pp. 154–155. No matter how the anthropology of Frazer may be disputed or may be antiquated, it remains a significant classic among those working in religious metaphor.

8. *Julian of Norwich: Showings,* trans. and intro. Edmund Colledge and James Walsh, Classics of Western Spirituality (New York: Paulist Press, 1978), p. 183.

9. Ibid. Although this nutshell experience does not appear in the short form of *Showings,* and although Julian has allegorized the three properties: that God made it, that God loves it, and that God preserves it, nevertheless, her reflection on the hazelnut resembles other mystical experiences of the "implosion" of nothingness.

CHAPTER 2

1. Julian Morgenstern, *The Ark, The Ephod, and The Tent of Meeting* (Cincinnati: Hebrew Union College Press, 1945).
2. The term "liminal" derives from Arnold van Gennep, referring to the borderline, marginal, "no-place" of persons passing from one societal status to another. This "invisible" quality has been fully developed by the work of Victor Turner. See, for example, *The Forest of Symbols: Aspects of Ndembu Ritual* (Ithaca, N.Y.: Cornell University Press, 1967), in Chapter IV: "Betwixt and Between: the Liminal Period in *Rites de Passage.*" There, Turner discusses symbolism of liminality: "This coincidence of opposite processes and notions in a single representation characterizes the peculiar unity of the liminal: that which is neither this nor that, and yet is both." p. 99. The "boxes," dreams, improvisations, stories of this work may be called the visible or notable formations—images, metaphors, archetypes, or symbols—of liminality, of discovering ourselves on edge, transforming our boundaries and ourselves.
3. Clark Wissler, *Ceremonial Bundles of the Blackfoot Indians. Anthropological Papers of the American Museum of Natural History.* Vol. VII, Part 2 (New York: Published by Order of the Trustees, 1912), p. 75.
4. However, this notion of secularization, as indicated in these pages may be inadequate to describe human culture in any of its forms. Mircea Eliade has said that "whatever modern, secularized man might think of himself, he still occupies a sacred dimension." And further that "the sacred is an element in the structure of human consciousness, that it is a part of the human mode of being in the world." "The Sacred in the Secular World," *Cultural Hermeneutics,* Vol. I, 1973, pp. 101–113.
5. *Meister Eckhart,* trans. Raymond Bernard Blakney (New York: Harper & Brothers, Publishers, 1941), p. 251. On pp. 252–253, "Meister Eckhart's Daughter" roughly parallels the "Beautiful Naked Boy," and both are particularly resonant with the discussion in Chapter 6.

CHAPTER 3

1. Lewis Carroll, *Through the Looking-Glass, and What Alice Found There* (New York: A Signet Classic from New American Library, 1960), Chapter V, pp. 171–172.
2. Plato, *Meno,* trans. Benjamin Jowett (New York: Library of Liberal Arts, The Bobbs-Merrill Company, Inc., 1949), 86b.

CHAPTER 5

1. Wallace Stevens, *The Collected Poems of Wallace Stevens* (New York: Alfred A. Knopf, 1954), p. 503.
2. Norman O. Brown, *Love's Body* (New York: Vintage Books, 1968), p. 261.
3. Examples of Reformationist zeal are readily found in art histories. One interesting story of iconoclastic ambivalence is told by Roland Bainton, *The Reformation of the Sixteenth Century* (Boston: Beacon Press, 1952), p. 84: "Popular

iconoclasm likewise commenced. That young Platter, who had been so exhilarated by Zwingli's preaching, stole a wooden image of St. John from the church, and when the caller came shoved the saint into the stove. The paint began to crackle. 'Keep still, Johnny,' muttered Platter."

CHAPTER 6

1. Philip Wheelwright, *Heraclitus* (New York: Atheneum, 1974, orig. pub. 1959), Fragment #21, p. 29, which reads specifically, "You cannot step twice into same river, for other waters are continually flowing on." Another fragment, #110, p. 90, reads the more paradoxical version, "Into the same rivers we step and do not step."
2. E. A. Speiser, trans., "Etana," in *Ancient Near Eastern Texts Relating to the Old Testament*, ed. James B. Pritchard (Princeton, New Jersey: Princeton University Press, 1969) p. 116. Versions of the Near Eastern myths mentioned in these pages can be found in this volume.
3. Kafka, *The Great Wall of China*, Reflection #13, p. 165.
4. Richard Burgin, *Conversations with Jorge Luis Borges* (New York: Avon Books, 1968). Epilogue. Borges' stories and witticisms are saturated with the image of the labyrinth.
5. Robert Graves, *The Greek Myths* (Baltimore, Maryland: Penguin Books, 1955), Volume I, p. 139.
6. James Joyce, *Finnegans Wake* (New York: Penguin Books, 1969, orig. pub. 1939), p. 104. Liberty was taken with spacing for the sake of context here.

CHAPTER 7

1. John Nance, *The Gentle Tasaday: A Stone Age People in the Philippine Rain Forest* (New York: Harcourt Brace Jovanovich, 1975), p. 118, perhaps in response to a leading question, Balayem suggests, "The soul may be the part of you that sees the dream" in the text is Balayem's statement from *National Geographic*, August, 1972, p. 243.
2. Homer, *The Odyssey*, trans. by Robert Fitzgerald (Garden City, N.Y.: Doubleday & Company, Inc., 1961), Book 24, line 13f.
3. Hesiod, *Theogony*, trans. and intro. Norman O. Brown (New York: The Bobbs-Merrill Company, Inc., 1953), p. 59.
4. Egyptian dream interpretation in *Hieratic Papyri in the British Museum. Third Series*, ed. by A. H. Gardiner (London: British Museum, 1935).
5. Naphtali Lewis, *The Interpretation of Dreams and Portents*, Aspects of Antiquity (Toronto: Samuel Stevens Hakkert & Company, 1976). Lewis also selects from the Egyptian material, above.
6. Wissler, *Ceremonial Bundles*, p. 101.
7. A. Leo Oppenheim, "Mantic Dreams in the Ancient Near East," in *The Dream and Human Societies*, ed. by Gustave E. von Grunebaum and Roger Callois (Berkeley: University of California Press, 1966), p. 350.
8. Genesis Rabbah 89:8. See David Bakan, *Sigmund Freud and the Jewish Mystical*

Tradition (New York: Schocken Books, 1965), who quotes from Freud's *The Interpretation of Dreams*, ". . . we have treated as Holy Writ what previous writers have regarded as an arbitrary improvisation. . . ." p. 251. And, Bakan points out, the principle in the Talmudic *Berakoth* is, "All dreams follow the mouth," that is, that interpretation had priority over the dream itself. Pp. 261–262.

9. Wheelwright, *Heraclitus*, Fragment #15, p. 20. Another of Heraclitus' aphorisms should be recalled as well: "Even sleepers are workers and collaborators in what goes on in the universe." Fragment #124, p. 102. The isolation and utter privacy of the first is tempered by the paradox of the philosopher's "hidden unity."

10. James Hillman, "Image-Sense," *Spring* (Irving, Texas, Spring Publications, Inc., 1979) pp. 130–143. Hillman concludes his essay: "Release from symbolic hermeneutics—'I must find out what the image means; interpretation, understanding.' Instead, aesthetics . . . It seems aesthetics is the *via regia*, if we would restore our life in images and work out the appropriate method for the poetic basis of mind, mind based in fantasy images." See especially his book *The Dream and the Underworld* (New York: Harper & Row, Publishers, 1979).

11. Artemidorus, *The Interpretation of Dreams*, trans. Robert White (Park Ridge, N.J.: Noyes Data Corp., 1975).